Perfect
Communications

OCTOBER 20, 1995
SINGAPORE

Perfect Communications

ALL YOU NEED
TO GET IT RIGHT
FIRST TIME

ANDREW LEIGH and
MICHAEL MAYNARD

ARROW
BUSINESS BOOKS

DEDICATION

To our families and friends, associates and clients –
keep talking!

This edition published by Arrow Books in 1994

10 9 8 7 6 5 4 3 2 1

Copyright © Andrew Leigh and Michael Maynard 1993

The right of Andrew Leigh and Michael Maynard
to be identified as the authors of this work has been asserted by them
in accordance with the Copyright, Designs and Patents Act, 1988

First published in Great Britain by
Century Business

Arrow Books Limited
Random House Ltd, 20 Vauxhall Bridge Road, London SW1V 2SA

Random House Australia (Pty) Limited
20 Alfred Street, Milsons Point, Sydney,
New South Wales 2061, Australia

Random House New Zealand Limited
18 Poland Road, Glenfield
Auckland 10, New Zealand

Random House South Africa (Pty) Limited
PO Box 337, Bergvlei, South Africa

Random House UK Limited Reg. No. 954009

A CIP catalogue record for this book
is available from the British Library

ISBN 0 7126 5602 2

Set in Bembo by
SX Composing Ltd., Rayleigh, Essex
Printed and bound in Great Britain by
Cox & Wyman Ltd, Reading, Berkshire

ABOUT THE AUTHORS

Andrew Leigh is the author of several successful books on decision making, management techniques and effective change, all published by the Institute of Personnel Management. He trained as an economist at the LSE, has an MA in Manpower Studies from London University and is a Fellow of the IPM. He started his career in marketing, and was for several years a business writer including three years on the business section of *The Observer*. He was a practising senior manager in the public services for many years.

Michael Maynard has led business and management workshops across the UK and in Europe, specializing in creativity, self-expression and communication skills. After receiving an honours degree in sociology from London University he had a successful career as an actor and presenter, and was a familiar face on TV. He has written for theatre, radio and TV and created many training videos. He has been a pioneer in using theatre techniques in education and business.

Andrew Leigh and Michael Maynard have together written *The Perfect Presentation*, another in this series of management guides, and *ACE Teams – creating star performance in business*, a book about team development. They run MAYNARD LEIGH ASSOCIATES the management development and consultancy service which works with many major British companies.

If you would like to communicate with them, they can be contacted at:

Maynard Leigh Associates
7 Rostrevor Mews
London SW6 5AZ

Tel: 071 371 5288
Fax: 071 371 5299

ACKNOWLEDGEMENT

Our special thanks to Adrienne Burgess for her assistance in the writing of this book.

CONTENTS

INTRODUCTION – GETTING STARTED

This is a book to use, not just to read. No need to plough on from here to the end. Just dip in and out, hunting for what seems usable, grabbing bits to try out.

We'll start with our final message from the end of *Perfect Communications*: practise. We are assuming you really want to improve your communications. If not, now's the time to close the book or give it to someone who needs it more.

Why does communication interest you right now? Have you felt for some time you could do better? Do you want some tips to use at work? Has someone suggested it would be a good idea to look at the topic?

Whatever your reasons, we offer you this written guarantee:

- You **can** improve your communication skills

We can say this, because over the years we have helped hundreds of people develop their communication abilities. In scores of workshops for both large and small organizations, we've never met anyone who couldn't improve if they were committed to doing so. This book distils many of the key ideas they have also found useful.

Scope
First, let's separate communication from a formal presentation. If the latter is your main concern you may wish to look at our *Perfect Presentation* book in this same series.

Perfect Communications goes far wider than presentations. 'Communications' is so broad a term it's easy to be confused by its scope. It potentially covers everything from conducting interviews to how the mail room works, from holding meetings to computer networks.

We've therefore narrowed it down to three broad areas: communicating face to face; dealing with what we've called 'the technology', which includes writing, phoning and handling the media; and finally the interpersonal areas of relationship building, handling conflict, and feedback.

At its core, communication is all about relating to other people. Its importance is hardly in doubt these days. If you're a manager, for example, you spend around half your time generating information and most of the remaining time using or dispensing it. In one form or another you speak, write, send information or just relate to other people. In fact your working day is probably spent mainly dealing with people.

Even if you are not a manager, communication plays an important part in your life. It's something everybody does. But communication is also about getting results. Results with other people. Since people are complicated beings, we can hardly expect communications to be any different.

You're an expert
Secondly, you are already an expert in communications. You already known an enormous amount about it because you've been doing it since birth.

So you also know there's a great difference between good and bad communications. You've certainly experienced both at some time. Let's jog your memory.

2

Exercise

Who have you met in recent years who seemed to have a problem with communications in some way? What was it?

Name: *Type of problem*

....

....

....

Now what about some good communicators you've met personally? Who are they? Can you sum up what impressed you?

Name: *Ability to:*

....

....

....

We asked you to do these two simple tasks because improving your communications abilities is partly about raising your awareness of what is happening around you. So we had a look at your existing awareness.

Much of the rest of this book will be helping you develop this awareness about what is happening, what does and doesn't work in communications.

Now consider the 24 hours before you picked up this book. Unless you were being a hermit, sitting alone at a computer screen or lost in the desert, you had many different communication experiences. What were they?

Exercise

Choose five communication events from the last 24 hours. It could have been a discussion with someone, a brief meeting, a phone call, talk and so on.

Now try reviewing them in terms of who was involved, the medium, the purpose and finally the result. What did you want or expect from the situation?

We've given an example to get you started:

Who?	Medium	Purposes	Result & Comment
Me and Pat	Phone	Clarify who is going to call the garage about fixing the car	Me! I just knew I'd end up doing it.

This apparently simple exercise allows you to begin dissecting what's currently happening with your own communications. Try it! Look at the results column. Did you get exactly what you wanted each time? If so, well done. You obviously make communication work well for you.

Maybe, though, not every event turned out quite how you wanted it. Or with hindsight, perhaps the purpose was not as clear as it should have been.

If you are with us so far, it's time to start with the first requirement of good communications: getting attention.

PART ONE

Face to Face

1

GETTING ATTENTION – PERFECT IMPACT

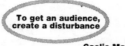

To get an audience, create a disturbance

Gaelic Maxim

WHY GET ATTENTION?

Attracting attention ensures what you say, your ideas, and your wishes, are all heard. It's therefore the first requirement for being a good communicator.

So you want to make an impact. How do you do it really well? And why are some people more memorable than others, communicating more effectively and getting their messages through every time?

The essence of gaining attention is taking care: caring about what you have to say; caring enough about yourself and others to be assertive and prepare your communication well; and taking care of those you are addressing.

Why bother? Some of the more obvious reasons are:

- You are more effective
- You keep people informed
- You involve others
- You get what you want
- You build relationships
- You achieve action

The rest of this guide is about ways of making this happen.

IS IT WHAT YOU REALLY WANT?

As you might expect, grabbing your share of attention does not come solely through wishful thinking. But really wanting to be a first-rate communicator and being willing to pay the price, is a great start.

It means putting yourself on the line and taking risks. How does that appeal? Many people are simply unwilling to go that far, either through fear or false modesty. Are you one of them? You may have to risk being

- attacked
- challenged
- ignored
- mocked

All of these can and do sometimes happen even to good communicators. They don't like it, any more than you do. Yet they are still willing to risk it, to step out and face whatever comes.

And while some people worry about their attention-getting going wrong, others have a different problem. They back away from praise and recognition, they shun the limelight which goes with excellent communicating. You may have to risk being

- congratulated
- promoted
- asked to follow through
- put in charge

Good communicators put up with these too. If you're ready to explore both the good consequences of getting attention and some of the downside, then this guide is for you.

Let's start with some of the basics of communicating.

THE BASICS
People who attract attention may seem to do it casually, without much effort. Don't be fooled. Careful planning

and preparation – not necessarily always conscious – goes into achieving it.

The basics of making an impact are focusing on:

- Your audience
- Your communication
- Yourself

YOUR AUDIENCE

'Getting attention' never happens in a vacuum. It's a two, three, or even four way process. Your audience must 'give' their attention, just as much as you must demand it. But why should they?

Whether you're speaking to a live audience, talking on the phone, interviewing someone, writing a report or a memo, merely 'sending' the information is not enough.

Good communicators realize all sorts of blocks can stop their message getting through.

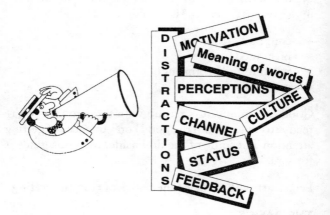

To get attention your audience must both receive and, equally important, understand your message. The two are not necessarily the same. Similarly you probably want your audience not to merely receive but also to:

● Accept and use your message.

To deal with the possible blocks it really helps to discover:

● who is the audience?
● what does it want?
● what does it fear?
● what does it care about?
● how could it be surprised?

Even as you are reading this you can probably think of some forthcoming communication situation in which you'd dearly like to succeed. Try applying the above five check questions right now:

Exercise

Situation (describe it in one sentence) ....

....

Who is the audience? _____

What does it want? _____

What does it fear? _____

What does it care about? _____

How could it be surprised? _____

Not every sort of attention is desirable. The kind you want is positive, which may not be obtained by shouting the loudest or wearing the brightest socks. Sometimes it's those who speak softest who make the strongest impression.

Successful actors, experts at gaining centre stage, frequently win attention by involving rather than dominating their audience.

YOUR COMMUNICATION

Which type of communication will best express your message? Would it best be achieved by a casual chat, meeting, interview, formal presentation, written report or what? Your chosen channel or method of communication can totally influence the success or failure of your attempt to gain attention.

Too many people choose the wrong channel and then wonder why they've failed to get through. For instance, some managers rely heavily on memos and written instructions when what's needed is personal contact and face to face communication. Others rely on a casual chat in the corridor when a more formal approach may be preferable. Decide what you most need and create it.

The more important your communication, the more helpful writing it down proves to be, even if ultimately you give your communication verbally. The next two chapters on GETTING IT DOWN and GETTING TO THE POINT help you both define and refine what you want to communicate.

When you have a first draft, you explore its attention-getting potential by reviewing:

- Is my opening communication arresting?
- Am I using memorable phrases or images?
- Am I writing, or speaking, from the heart (see GETTING REAL below)
- Am I appealing to their feelings and their minds?
- Is my written material professionally presented (smart folder, good print etc)

- Could visuals (cartoons, photographs etc.) add impact?
- Does my communication contain the unexpected?
- Could humour get more attention?

REHEARSAL

If your communication is verbal, and you're satisfied with the basic outline, stand up and rehearse it aloud. Even if eventually you will be talking while sitting, or sending written material, rehearsing it aloud while standing focuses your attention and energy on the communication.

Rehearse it again. And again . . . Skimp on rehearsals and however impressive you appear, however good your ideas, *you will not be maximizing your impact.*

The point of most communication is to share your view of the world. So for maximum impact, try to help people experience that view, make it real for them. Use examples, images, anecdotes and case studies, so that your audience can picture what you mean.

YOUR AUDIENCE – AGAIN

Once your communication is well prepared and rehearsed, it's time to think about your AUDIENCE again. Throughout this guide we will keep returning to the audience.

What are the likely objections to what you have to say? Have good answers prepared. Do more research if necessary.

Where negotiations are involved, know your own boundaries. For instance, what are your terms and how far are you willing to compromise? And since making an impact can demand further action, become clear on what this might mean: what are you willing, and able, to take on? Consolidate the good impression you make with effective follow-up.

YOURSELF AS MEDIUM

Getting attention and making an impact is not an event – it's a process. You are part of it and the person through whom the message is transmitted. Or as media expert Marshall McLuhan put it:

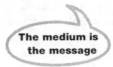

The medium is the message

So getting attention means preparing both your mind and body.

KNOWING YOURSELF

The person who makes the greatest impact is usually someone who is most him or herself. Children and animals are always thoroughly themselves – and consequently 'steal the scene'. Being just themselves they seldom transmit 'mixed messages'.

Mixed messages make an audience feel unsafe – as if they can't quite believe their eyes or ears. So, for instance, only go for power-dressing if you already feel powerful. Or only push daring ideas which you fully understand and when you can get completely behind them. Audiences soon detect when you are saying, or writing, one thing but really meaning something else.

LIKING YOURSELF

If you don't believe you have something valuable to communicate why should anyone else? So, if necessary, be willing to work on your self-esteem; it may be crucial. Here are three exercises to help you build self-confidence.

Exercise I

Make a list of all your achievements – all the things you've accomplished and of which you're proud. Make it as long as you like.

Now list all the skills you've developed on the way. Include everything from swimming badges to helping somebody, from exams to riding a bicycle, from great meals you've cooked to getting your present job. Make it a long list.

It's important to recognize what you have to offer. You may take these accomplishments for granted, but others might find them impressive.

Exercise 2

List your essential qualities as a human being. This can give you a sense of who you are.

Ask: what's distinctive about me? Canvass five friends to say what they think makes you who you are.

Exercise 3

Imagine future communications as if you were watching them on TV or a film screen. 'See' them going brilliantly, exactly as you would wish. Play this positive story regularly in your mind, as many times as you can throughout the day.

YOUR BODY/YOURSELF

Having encouraged your internal self, it's time to consider how your physical presence can contribute to getting attention.

The Perfect Presentation, our other book in this same series, can help you make the best use of your voice and appearance. Learning to relax is also important. How do truly confident people behave? Generally they take it

13

for granted that they will gain attention when they need it. They no longer try hard to impress, they know they do anyway.

So a useful tip for using your physical appearance to gain attention is:

- Act as if you already have their attention

When you behave as if you are already centre stage, in the limelight and focused intently on your audience, your body does the rest. No need or time to worry about your hands, your height, your big feet, your funny hair or whatever gets in the way of making an impact.

If you rely for impact on a fabulous Filofax, a great car and super-boss clothes, you will be relying on props rather than the real you. We are not suggesting you slop into the room wearing any old comfortable clobber. Clothes and accessories should contribute to making you feel good, yet need to be appropriate to the situation. When they are, they help you gain your share of attention. Above all, they should show signs of care – caring for yourself and your audience.

Exercise
   a) *Look at yourself in the mirror. Do you look cared for, as if you look after yourself?*
   b) *If you are not confident about your clothes and general image try asking someone whose style you admire to help you renew your wardrobe. People love to give advice and feel flattered if you seek their help on something as personal as clothes and appearance. You may even want to consult an expert.*

MAKING YOUR ENTRANCE
You begin to 'get attention' long before you enter the room. There will be an approach – up in the lift maybe, along the corridor, through the main office.

You won't claim the right sort of attention if you behave as if you have an 'on-off' switch. There's no point, for instance, in suddenly turning on a relaxed air as you enter, if the boss's Personal Assistant previously saw you anxiously chewing your lip in reception. He or she may mention this later and undermine your apparently confident front.

When you enter the room you already feel sufficiently comfortable about yourself to give your whole attention to your audience. It's not just what you 'put out' that matters, its also what you 'take in' that's crucial.

There's always a relationship – a 'chemistry' – between communicators and their audience. People who receive well for example, that is good listeners, are often those who make the most powerful impact.

It is as important for a good manager to know how to listen as well as to talk. We too often forget that communication is an exchange

Lee Iacocca

Example

Several candidates for a top director's job were interviewed by the staff as part of the selection process. Most candidates entered the room and rapidly embarked on an explanation of what they would do for the company. One woman though began by explaining that she'd prefer to hear from each of those present about their vision of the future. Later she responded with her views too, having established herself as being a listener and not always pushing her own ideas. She was appointed to the job.

THE CURTAIN RISES ...

So here you are – hoping to 'get attention' through some kind of direct personal communication. You feel good about yourself and the way you look. You're well rehearsed. You have something important to say and know why you're saying it.

You enter the room and the temptation is to go for it right away – to burst forth with your communication. Getting attention, though, is about being aware of where the attention already is, and moving it gently round to where you want it.

'Take in' the person (or people) you have come to see. Are they just putting down the telephone? Or deeply absorbed in discussion? If so, making an impact will involve bringing them back to where you are, putting them in the frame of mind to receive your message.

ASSERTION

People who attract the right kind of attention act *assertively* when communicating with others. Being assertive is not about being aggressive, dominating or winning. Nor is it a 'trick' with which to manipulate others.

Both words and body language signal to your audience whether or not you are being assertive. For example, if you shake hands with someone as you enter the room, is your grip like a limp rag, or is it firm and solid? Limp handshakes can undermine your communication just as much as a limp speech. Having said that, we are not suggesting you grip the other person in a vice-like squeeze which leaves them wincing.

Being assertive means:

● Saying directly what you want, need or feel, but *not* at the expense of other people

- Behaving in a rational and adult way
- Being able to negotiate and reach workable compromises
- Insisting on being heard, even if you have to keep repeating your message
- Knowing you deserve respect and acting accordingly
- Showing you have purpose

Above all, assertiveness is about being honest – with yourself and others.

Example

A young woman attending a finalists' interview for Young Businesswoman of the Year found herself gabbling nervously early in the interview. 'I'm sorry', she said, 'this is very important to me, and I feel nervous. I just need to stop for a minute and breathe'. With that, she took several calm deep breaths – and smiled before resuming her reply. She won the award.

COMPLETION

Once you have attracted attention you must maintain it. Every letter we despatch, every memo we send, every communication we make is an expression of who we are.

And either who you are is important – or it is not. When it is, then you will get attention.

Every piece of work we do is a self portrait; autograph your work with excellence

2

GETTING TO THE POINT: PERFECT SPOKEN COMMUNICATION

Take care of the sense and the sounds will take care of themselves

Lewis Carroll, *Alice's Adventures in Wonderland*

Perfect spoken communication is about expressing exactly what we think, feel and want, so our listeners understand.

The more concise, clear and specific we are, the better. It's our responsibility to get the message across. It's no use blaming the other person – we need to find the language they can hear.

It's easy to spoil communication, if you are:

- A Know-all: always goes one better, with an answer for everything

- An Interrupter: hardly listens, prepares to talk while the other is talking; cuts people short

- A Rambler: babbles about nothing just to stay the centre of attention

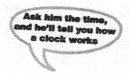

Ask him the time, and he'll tell you how a clock works

- A Solo-Artist: talks non-stop, asking and answering own questions and laughing at own jokes

There was nothing wrong with her that a vasectomy of the vocal cords wouldn't fix

Lisa Alther, *Kinflicks*

- An Egotist: 'I . . . I . . . I', boosts self-esteem by boasting about self

Ted Turner, Founder of Cable Network News

If only I had a little humility, I'd be perfect

- A Bore: talks endlessly on matters of no interest to anyone but the talker

Somebody's boring me - I think it's me

Dylan Thomas

- A Dumper: claims to be useless or guilty yet won't offer to alter behaviour

- A Blamer: tells listeners unpleasant home truths 'for their own good'

- A Whisperer: speaks every sentence confidentially; it's a strain to hear

- A Joker: reduces everything to a funny one-liner; it's wearing

- A Moaning Minnie: constantly complains, and the whole world is to blame

We hope you are none of these. However, try asking some trusted friends and colleagues to describe your communication style.

Speaking

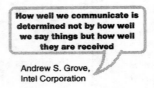

How well we communicate is determined not by how well we say things but how well they are received

Andrew S. Grove,
Intel Corporation

Key points to help you achieve what you want are:

- Speak up and speak out: whether chatting to a colleague by the photocopier or addressing a meeting it's essential people hear you.

  Your listener's ear is much further from your mouth than your own. If the listener is slightly hard of hearing, and many people are, help them by turning your face towards them.

It's your responsibility to make yourself heard. You need to do the work, not the listener.

- Use simple concrete language: express your ideas through facts, examples and anecdotes. Don't be afraid to rephrase until your listener understands.

  Be sparing in using verbal shorthand or jargon.

- Use space, not fillers: Identify your favourite fillers, all the 'umms, ers, y'knows' and so on. Name them with the help of your friends

  Having recognized your fillers, watch out for when you use them and replace them with . . .

  . . . nothing.

Use silence. It leaves space for both of you to experience what is said and what is happening between you

Drawing on my fine command of language, I said nothing

Robert Benchley

- Be direct: Avoid rambling instead of saying simply what you think or what you want.

  For example: 'Do you think it might possibly be a good idea, if I were to perhaps . . . well, I was wondering whether . . . if we all agreed, maybe we should . . .'

  Often embarrassment prevents us from speaking our minds simply and directly. If you feel embarrassed, notice it, acknowledge it to yourself and still speak simply and directly.

- Be specific: vagueness causes confusion.

  For example: 'The technology in this place is always going wrong, it's useless' is less likely to get action than 'The photocopier has broken down for the fourth time this week.'

- Full Stop: use the full stop principle; instead of restating the same point, make it . . . then stop.

Beware of using subordinate clauses – sentences within sentences – and too many examples, when the person has already got your point.

Check they've understood, and . . . Full Stop.

- Avoid unnecessary detail: kill the waffle. Get to the

point and stay there. Keep reminding yourself of the purpose of your communication.

● Use the first person when speaking – that means saying 'I' rather than 'You', 'We' or 'One'. For example, 'I think', 'I feel', 'I find'.

Before communicating with others, how about communicating with yourself, so your speech reflects clear understanding and purpose? (see GETTING REAL)

If you have scope to plan, ask yourself:

● What is my main message?
● Why am I saying it?
● Who is it for?
● What outcome do I want?
● Are the facts correct?
● Have I left anything out?
● Is the required action clear?

If you have doubts about yourself and your communication you will certainly somehow reveal it. Your listeners will feel they cannot trust you and this will undermine your message. So it is worth preparing for any important communication.

Also prepare your listener:

● Agree time and place
● Arouse curiosity
● Check willingness to communicate
● Review assumptions
● Outline the subject
● Describe its importance
● Summarize the benefits

Successful spoken communications are productive.

They improve the quality of life by helping people to achieve, to know useful information, to feel happier or more content.

So it's seldom productive to make personal attacks or to make a listener defensive. You may win the battle yet lose the war.

There is also a danger of taking too much responsibility. Do you feel it's up to you to fix every problem that emerges? Sometimes simply allowing the other person to express confusion, disappointment, anger or sadness is enough. If anything needs changing they may well find their own answers.

First step
Improving how you speak and get to the point is a matter of practice. The first step is awareness, knowing what is working and what is not.

You can start checking how you speak by asking friends and colleagues for feedback. Ideally you have to catch yourself unawares, when you are being natural. Try the following exercise:

Exercise
With the permission of colleagues tape-record a meeting in which you are taking part. Explain that it's purely to examine your own communication skills.

Later listen to the recording, alone. Examine how you contributed to the meeting, particularly how quickly and easily you got to the point. How could you do it better next time?

Over the top
The suggestions in this chapter can help develop your ability to get to the point. However, there's always a danger of overdoing it, becoming a person who justifies

their rudeness with comments like: 'I don't mince my words; I come straight to the point; People can take it or leave it.'

While sometimes refreshing, such frankness can also be blunt and insensitive. The priority is to care for your listener and assess the moment-by-moment response to what you are saying.

3

GETTING THE MESSAGE ACROSS: PERFECT GROUP COMMUNICATION

What is a perfect group communicator? Is it a brilliant chair person, a superb speaker, an arch manipulator, an ideas supplier or what? How can you become more effective in a group so that your message always comes across?

We're not talking here about formal presentations or how to run a meeting. You can read about these in other books in this series.

Here we're concentrating on what produces good communications *within* a group. The focus is on being effective at improving the entire group communications process, and in doing so getting your own message through.

Any gathering of two or more people is a group. In team meetings, committees or boardrooms the individuals share a common past, present and future. They mesh together through a constantly changing network of interests. Effective group communicators take this into account.

Occasionally, as in a public meeting, a one-off conference or a first-time gathering for a specific purpose, the group consists of people without much or any knowledge of one another. Again, being aware of what happens on such occasions can enable you to improve the general communication process.

Good communicators know it's worth becoming aware of how groups work, because they behave differently from individuals. They develop their own personalities and ways of operating.

GROUP STAGES

How do groups develop? They pass through recogniz-able stages of forming, storming, norming, performing and mourning. Each suggests a different communica-tion approach:

- Forming: people get together. They reveal and check out limits, review purpose and explore ex-pectations
- Storming: people compete for position, test limits, explore possibilities and come to understand one another. This phase can involve rebellion and as-sertion
- Norming: people agree on collective behaviour (norms), shared values and take responsibility. Now you discover what you can and can't do within this group
- Performing: the members cooperate to achieve common goals and may both work and play to-gether and nurture one another
- Mourning: end of the group, people withdraw and clear up any unfinished business before leaving

IMPLICATIONS

What are the implications of these five stages? The first is the value of recognizing the current stage of group de-velopment. Then you can gear your communication appropriately. Detect the stage by looking carefully for the signs already described.

Secondly, the five stages suggest slightly different con-tributions from you.

- Forming: awareness of the formation process means encouraging discussion on issues such as:
  - Why are we here?
  - What's our real purpose?
  - What holds us firmly together?
  - What are we prepared to do and NOT do together?

- What are our rules for working together?
- What do we expect from one another?
- How will people outside this group respond to us?
- What's the best and worst that could happen if we continue down this route together?

Exercise

To speed up the 'forming' phase of group development, everyone sits in a circle. In turn people introduce themselves and say why they are in the group and what they hope to get from it. Then they say what special skills or experience they bring to the group.

- Storming: during this stage, which can be exciting and difficult, encourage group communication around issues such as:

   - What role is each of us to play?
   - Shall we have a formal leader or chairperson?
   - Who wants to become the leader?
   - Who do we want as leader?
   - What powers shall we give our formal leader?
   - How do we resolve conflict if several people want to lead?
   - Do we encourage disagreement and people expressing a difference of opinion?
   - How will we resolve differences between us – for example by compromise, or formal voting?
   - What happens if someone refuses to conform to the group's wishes?
   - How do we deal with strong feelings – for example making space to air them?

Exercise

To speed up the 'storming' stage, alternate timed periods of 'free-for-all' discussion with periods where each person gets an allotted solo spot – to speak individually.

- Norming: during this phase contribute to good communications by helping people realize:

  - What are our formal rules?
  - What are our usually unspoken rules – for example, that no one interrupts you when you are speaking?
  - Who has what formal role – for example who will take the minutes?
  - How far can people challenge the group in some way?
  - How do we deal with differences of opinion?
  - How far can an individual follow his or her own interests at the expense of the group?

Exercise

To get the most out of the 'norming' stage, spend some time exchanging information about personal interests, favourite music, books or places. It will help the group to arrive at shared interests and values.

- Performing: now you can help the communication process by focusing on:

  - What are our specific targets or goals?
  - How are we setting about achieving them?
  - Who has what detailed responsibilities and do they understand these?
  - Can we make being together more rewarding – for example by having fun together, socializing, recognizing one another's successes?
  - How best can we support people through difficult times?
  - Are we listening to one another properly?
  - Does each speaker build on what the previous person has said?
  - Do we give each other and the group regular feedback?

    – Who is showing high or low commitment to group aims?

Exercise

To improve the 'performing' stage, celebrate successes and be determined to grow. Take part in adventures together, like setting yourselves outrageous challenges and trying to achieve them.

- Mourning: when the group is ending, help group communications by encouraging attention to issues such as:

  - When do we stop meeting?
  - Who should we tell?
  - What remains to do before the last meeting?
  - Who takes responsibility for post-group matters – for example handling residual assets or remaining tasks?
  - What do people feel about the group coming to an end?
  - How do we handle these feelings – for example having a reunion in a year, organizing a final party, sending a final report?
  - Could we make the ending into a celebration?

Exercise

To encourage the 'mourning' stage, get every person in the group to do a two-minute presentation of what they feel they got out of the project. Present it in an entertaining way, as a gift to the rest of the group.

BEING HEARD

For a group to be communicating well, it means that:

- everyone who needs to express an opinion does so
- subjects are fully explored

- the group takes care of all its members
- each person gets his or her message through to everyone
- the group produces action which is clear to all

How can you help these happen, especially if you are not always the group's formal leader? Often, it's by contributing, rather than waiting for others to take the lead.

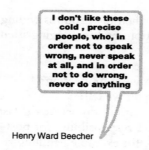

I don't like these cold , precise people, who, in order not to speak wrong, never speak at all, and in order not to do wrong, never do anything

Henry Ward Beecher

All groups have several kinds of leader:

- the responsible leader – the accountable person
- the effective leader – the person whose ideas are usually taken up
- the psychological leader – with whom group members are most likely to identify

Sometimes these qualities are all invested in the same person. More often they are split or the leadership moves around. Yet whenever you speak, for that moment you become the group leader.

Be a leader in meetings - even those you don't chair

Thomas L. Quick

There are several ways you can aid a group to solve problems, be more creative, and thus develop its communications:

- Encourage the group to select obstacles which are surmountable
- Demand facts, even when these are inadequate
- Push for people to explore problems thoroughly, rather than rushing to immediate solutions
- Encourage a distinction between developing ideas and the next stage of evaluating them, because the latter inhibits the former
- Where a group is facing a choice, help turn it into a problem-solving opportunity
- Where a group is facing a problem help convert it into a choice opportunity.

JOINING A GROUP

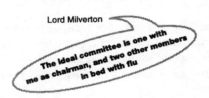

Lord Milverton

The ideal committee is one with me as chairman, and two other members in bed with flu

When you are part of a group make an effort to communicate well from the outset. It will help you feel included:

- Learn everyone's names; if necessary sketch on a piece of paper where people are sitting and add names as you hear them
- Greet people
- Move around the group during breaks, introducing yourself and learning about the other people
- Reveal your own cares and concerns

If you have hidden reasons for joining the group or little

in common with most members, communication will not be open or easy. There may be little point in trying to take part.

GETTING YOUR MESSAGE ACROSS

You need to be flexible to get your message across in a group. While you should have a clear sense of purpose, your 'message' need not be clear at the start. Too fixed a view may, in fact, inhibit real communication. However, you should be able to hold to your view if you believe you are right, and even enjoy being challenged because it allows you to refine your argument.

Controlling or manipulative behaviour may, in the short term, get your message across or get what you want. But long term, openly asserting your views allows them to be explored thoroughly. Good group communication happens when all members of the group and the leader(s) in particular:

- assume responsibility for accurate communication
- are sensitive to silence and unexpressed feelings
- do not read all silence as agreement
- urge the participation of those who have not yet spoken
- protect minority points of view
- keep the discussion moving
- develop skills in summarizing
- create a climate for disagreement which permits innovation
- promote problem-solving by encouraging people to:

  - search for and present ideas
  - listen to understand rather than to disagree
  - make short speeches

- keep a balance between problem-centred and

solution-centred communication – staying long
enough, but not too long, on the former.
- confront problems openly, for example
unmasking dishonest behaviour such as denial of
anger

Exercise
*Assess your behaviour within a group using the above
points.*
What are your strengths and skills?

GIVING AND RECEIVING

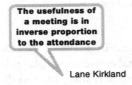

The usefulness of
a meeting is in
inverse proportion
to the attendance

Lane Kirkland

How well you communicate within a group depends in
large part on your skill at building relationships (see
GETTING ACQUAINTED). One of the greatest
gifts you give a group is to voice your concerns.

Do not apologize for your stupidity or worry that you
are holding the group up. Almost every time you will
find you are also speaking for other, less forthright,
group members.

Exercise
*Each member of the group holds a piece of paper: the
names of the group members appear in the left-hand
column; three empty columns across the page are headed
'MORE' 'LESS' and 'NO CHANGE'; next to each
name (except your own) write a phrase to describe what
you would like 'more of' (such as 'joining in') and 'less of'
(such as 'pushing us') from your colleagues – and what
you would like maintained (such as 'playfulness').*

33

Now pair with everyone in turn and discuss your findings. Make a note of what everyone wants of you. During these pairings you may wish to negotiate with some people and agree how to assess what happens.

CONFORMITY

The enemy of good group communications is conformity. Groups exert pressure on people to adapt to group standards or norms. These are the unwritten expectations which tell members what to do.

While conformity can help produce a useful consensus and even good joint working, it also prevents healthy disagreement and creativity, and can blind a group to reality.

The most dangerous form of conformity is Groupthink, where total consensus replaces honest communication and testing of reality. Instead the group thinks as a unit, is impervious to outside criticism and begins to believe itself invincible.

Many computer and military projects have suffered from Groupthink with members unable to communicate their true concerns about the size, cost, or feasibility of schemes. People often feel too much is at stake to backtrack.

While you alone may be unable to prevent Groupthink, here are some steps to improve communications and make it less likely:

- Encourage people to express doubts and criticisms or proposed solutions to problems
- Show by example you are willing to accept criticism
- Encourage the group to break into smaller groups to consider ideas and then meet to examine how they differ

- Suggest outsiders join the group and provide suggestions
- Alert people to potential Groupthink by saying for example: 'I feel we're being too keen to think as one on this. Does anyone have a different perspective on it?'

4

GETTING REAL: PERFECT HONESTY

FROM THE HEART

Speaking with conviction, from the heart, is communication at its finest. When we believe completely in what we say, we make a powerful impact: we persuade, inspire, convince and others respond to our calls to action.

Honest conviction has an attraction beyond the intellect. Through it, heart speaks to heart.

How is it achieved? Those who speak with conviction:

- know what they care about
- know what they fear
- know what they want
- let passion, will and mind work together
- are choosers, not victims

VICTIM OR CHOOSER?

The buck stops here

Harry S. Truman

We are responsible for the way we handle every situation – and, in most cases, even for the situation itself. Not recognizing this, we often turn into victims, which makes it hard for us to be honest with ourselves.

Choosers communicate honestly with themselves – and others. A chooser:

- works hard yet has more time

- goes straight to the problem
- knows when to fight hard and when to give way
- feels strong enough to be friendly
- listens
- respects others' strengths
- welcomes feedback
- explains
- feels responsible for more than his or her own work
- is willing to make mistakes
- focuses on possibilities and solutions

A victim:

- is always too busy
- goes round the problem
- promises too readily
- gives way on important issues, holds on to things that aren't worth fighting for
- can be a petty tyrant
- focuses on others' weaknesses
- resists feedback
- makes excuses
- says 'that's not my job'
- is afraid of making mistakes
- focuses on problems and insoluble issues

TALKING PASSION

When you are moved by your subject you automatically become a powerful communicator. Somehow you must find the passion, no matter how obscure the source.

By passion we do not necessarily mean, wild, sexual emotions or feverish romantic concerns. Passion occurs when you put your whole self into what you want to communicate. It's when you find a spark to ignite your message.

Look at your own area of work or business. To which part of it do you feel personally connected? It could be a product or service – or the concept behind it, doing things well, quickly, better or whatever. It might be satisfaction from the relationships you build, or the quality of the work.

Or perhaps you could dedicate part of your profits or earnings to some cause about which you care deeply. Look deeply or broadly enough and you'll find a source of honest inspiration in just about anything. When you find that source, you know why you are communicating – you speak with conviction and people 'hear' you.

Example

In growing The Body Shop, Anita Roddick was initially passionate about selling cosmetics and fragrances without elaborate packaging and hype. Then development of the empire itself became her driving concern. More recently, her inspiration is the difference her business can make in the community – and worldwide.

Exercise

Imagine you had enough money to be financially secure. How would you like to spend the day? Is there part of your present work you'd like to continue doing? Is there any relationship between reality and your wishes? If you find meaning in part of the work only, explore how you can build on this. When nothing in your daily work offers inspiration, be honest – it's time to move on.

MAKING TIME FOR THE TRUTH

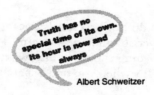

Truth has no special time of its own. Its hour is now and always

Albert Schweitzer

To summarize what we have been saying so far:

- Before you can expect to be a perfect communicator with others, you must develop honest
  communications with yourself. That takes time.
  Time dedicated not to doing but to being.

Example

*A young executive went to New York for a potentially
life-changing interview. If he got the job there were many
pros and cons to consider. Did he want it, should he take
it? A close colleague advised him to make the two-day trip
to New York by train, taking with him no writing or
reading materials. That journey changed his life. Freed
from his normal search for facts and conducting endless
analysis, his thoughts at first went in circles. The long
journey and nothing to do, led him to an easy certainty. It
gave him time to discover who he was and what he
wanted.*

Communicating honestly with yourself is different
from those frantic, whirling thoughts that preoccupy us
at five o'clock in the morning. When you contact yourself honestly, it is a calm, enriching experience that can
contribute powerfully to your external communications.

There are many ways to make this important form of
personal contact with yourself. Most of all you need to
set aside a special time for it. Some people think things
through during regular physical exercise – jogging,
working out, swimming. Others use meditation or
prayer for a similar purpose.

Exercise

*Create some private 'contemplation' time. Make it a
priority. This could be a few days away from it all, or
short gaps in the day's activity.*

Spending time on yourself is not self-indulgent or a waste of time, it's a solid investment in building your total communication powers

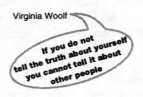

Virginia Woolf

If you do not tell the truth about yourself you cannot tell it about other people

We are not necessarily 'thinking for ourselves' when we think. Replayed in our heads are old tape recordings – voices of our father, mother, those who taught us to think as we do – and who now argue inside our heads. No wonder effective communication with others needs us to first recognize our own voice among so many.

Luckily we always provide clues for ourselves, if we are smart enough to see them:

- pay attention to thoughts which repeatedly 'pop up' which make you anxious or wish to ignore them

- try out your thoughts and ideas on other people (sometimes simply airing views is enough. At other times, feedback can be useful – see also GETTING BETTER, below)

- put your thoughts down on paper – asking and providing written answers to questions such as 'why am I in this situation?' 'what do I want?' 'what do I care about?'

- When facing a decision list the 'pros' and 'cons'

GETTING IN TOUCH
Sometimes we cannot 'get real' or 'become clear' because unacknowledged emotions are in the way. A constant flux of powerful feelings is part of being

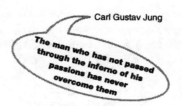

Carl Gustav Jung

The man who has not passed through the inferno of his passions has never overcome them

human, but as children we frequently learn to suppress or disregard them. Perhaps someone frowned on our excitement or rejected our expressions of pain or fear.

How can you discover what your real feelings are at any given moment? Partly by listening to that inner voice, the one that is the real you. Some useful ways to hear it are:

- note the words to songs which you find yourself humming involuntarily. Often they express emotions you dare not feel openly

- jot down what you can remember of your dreams on a pad kept by the bed. Think about them – the meaning will often reveal itself

- pay attention to what you disapprove of about other people. Often what disturbs you about them is what disturbs you about yourself

- if you always feel angry, or others always appear inept, are you worried or frightened about something?

- if you are always fearful and unwilling to assert yourself, could you be angry about something and suppressing it?

- if you feel extreme boredom are you repressing strong emotions about something?

Exercise

Keep a note of items on television or in the papers that excite you – to anger, joy, sadness and so on. Make a list of day-to-day activities which do the same. Are you allowing your feelings expression in daily life.

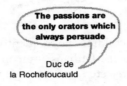

The passions are the only orators which always persuade

Duc de
la Rochefoucauld

FACT OR FEELING

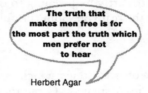

The truth that makes men free is for the most part the truth which men prefer not to hear

Herbert Agar

Strong feelings are useful, yet sometimes obscure your power to see life clearly. When feelings are becoming overpowering, try listing all the hard facts at your disposal. This can clear the emotional smoke screen and make it easier to communicate first with yourself and then with others.

Similarly when you are rich in facts and surrounded by hard evidence this could be an appropriate signal to explore how you are feeling about the situation. Facts too can be a smoke screen.

Since there are always both facts and feelings involved, if you want to speak with conviction watch out for the temptation to be excessively reasonable when anger, excitement or sorrow might be more appropriate.

PART TWO

Through the Technology

GETTING IT DOWN – PERFECT WRITTEN COMMUNICATION

Written communication is more difficult than, say, a meeting face-to-face. We have no control over you the reader. We want to grab and keep your attention. If we were physically together you'd find it hard to slip away. Yet we only have a set of symbols on a page.

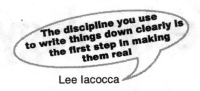

The discipline you use to write things down clearly is the first step in making them real

Lee Iacocca

When you send any form of written communication you are trusting in symbols, hoping for the best. Yet you can improve your chances of making them achieve results and this chapter explains how.

IN ESSENCE
Perfect written communication begins when you say exactly what you want, succinctly, and effectively. Clarity earns respect and persuades, because what you write is usually interesting or pleasant to read.

Write well and your message has impact. People do more than just read, note and file it. They respond.

Another gain from good written communications is fewer wasted meetings. Written communications let you contact many people simultaneously and therefore promote your ideas and action. Yet it's rarely as powerful as being physically there yourself.

EXPLORING YOUR SUBJECT
A well tried way to develop a topic and open areas for discussion is to ask 'open' questions – beginning with

words like WHAT, WHY, WHEN, HOW, WHERE or WHO.

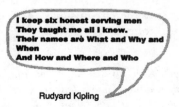

I keep six honest serving men
They taught me all I knew.
Their names are What and Why and When
And How and Where and Who

Rudyard Kipling

This technique can prompt you with ideas for, say, an article or letter; or a list of chapters for a longer piece.

Example

> *PROBLEM/SOLUTION*
> *What is the problem?*
> *When did it arise?*
> *What are the causes?*
> *How important are they?*
> *What are the preferred options?*
> *Why?*
> *Who needs to be involved?*

KEEP IT HUMAN

Today even report-writing is changing. Passive, impersonal statements like

'It was agreed that . . .'
'A complaint was made by the client'

are increasingly made active and personal:

'We agreed that . . .'

'The client complained . . .'

Spotting passive verbs is quite a skill. Low cost computer-based checkers like Stylewriter, mentioned more fully later, help to do it instantly.

People used to make a fuss about the differences between 'written' and 'spoken' English – that is, formal versus informal language. This too is changing. Except in the most extreme circumstances try for an almost conversational tone in your writing.

Exercise

When you have written what you think is your final draft, try reading it into a tape recorder. If you quickly become bored, that's how your reader may also respond.

Mark up complicated or awkward phrases as you read. Now play the recording, imagining your readership listening to it. Is your text something they would find easy to hear? Mark up problem areas and change them.

Report-writers can learn a lot from thriller-writers who need to master the art of suspense. With every paragraph your aim should be to hook in the reader and make it attractive to continue reading.

Ways to achieve this include:

- Early in your document create a challenge: 'what would happen/how would we cope if . . . ?'
- Ask 'rhetorical' questions – answering them yourself in the next paragraph
- Drop clues and hints before giving the total picture
- Head each section with arresting titles
- Stress topics in which readership is interested

Guidelines

Author Somerset Maugham once explained that there were three rules for writing a novel: 'unfortunately, no one knows what they are.' For most written communications, though, certain basic guidelines work.

- Know your message

- Know your audience
- Structure your material
- Be brief
- Summarize
- Present it attractively
- Supply facts
- Make numbers comparative
- Avoid jargon, remove clichés
- Use graphics
- Give conclusions or recommendations

Let's start putting these to work in your writing.

KNOW YOUR MESSAGE

Sounds obvious, doesn't it? Yet communication often fails because senders are unclear about their message. You should know:

- What do I want to say?
- Why do I want to say it?
- Why is it important – to me and to them?

Busy managers often forget the last of these. Concerned to state their message, they forget to explain why it should claim attention. Giving people a clear idea of why your message is important helps them decide their response.

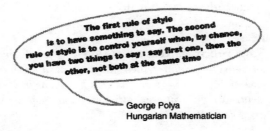

The first rule of style is to have something to say. The second rule of style is to control yourself when, by chance, you have two things to say : say first one, then the other, not both at the same time

George Polya
Hungarian Mathematician

KNOW YOUR AUDIENCE

Back to the audience again. Doing background research dramatically improves your chances of a communication succeeding.

Does the audience need:

fact	comfort
opinion	censure
inspiration	support
instruction	entertainment

Is the audience:

conventional	young
unconventional	sophisticated
educated	unsophisticated
uneducated	open to humour
old	hungry for facts

Will the audience:

understand your subject	see it as threatening
find it interesting	want to know more
grasp the essentials	need telling what to do

STRUCTURE

The core of a perfect communication is structure, or framework. This is how you arrange the different parts of the whole message. Use it to tell your 'story', and help your audience with its logic and flow.

Example

Script writers, directors and others trying to raise money for films often compress their structures into a 100-word or one-minute spoken story-line. It's known as high treatment. A high treatment story gets its message across in just a few brief sentences.

Try condensing your message and structure to just 100 words – even if you never use it on your audience. Reduce it even further and imagine a newspaper headline for it. With the essence of your written communication you lay a foundation for any longer version. Many companies, for instance, have improved communications by insisting no memo may exceed half a page.

With a sound framework you are half way to a perfect written communication. Are you working in an organization with its own rigid format or house style? Before blindly following it, be sure to understand its purpose.

Try asking those for whom you are writing whether any long-standing format still suits their needs. Companies follow unsatisfactory blueprints for years only because no one has questioned them. Make any challenge a tactful one.

Effective written structures usually have three sections:

- *introduction*
  a statement about, or illustration of, the theme

- *development*
  exploration of the theme

- *conclusion*
  summing-up – which may include a call to action

Some people believe in writing the conclusion first to clarify the rest of the material. You may choose to develop your document in a more logical sequence. Do what feels right for you. Just give your structure a form which people can quickly understand and use.

How can I know what I think till I see what I say?

E.M.Forster
(rejecting the maxim: 'Never begin a sentence until you know how to end it.')

Management reports need a proper structure such as this successful one:

> Management Summary (maximum 2 pages)
> Introduction
> Background analysis or body of report
> Conclusions
> Recommendations
> Appendix

Management reports of more than 15–20 pages are usually too long. If you write this much, always add an index page immediately after the management summary. It may also be helpful to briefly explain your structure in the introduction.

While on the subject of management reports, here are six productive techniques we've used for writing scores of successful reports:

> Start with a one-page summary
> Distinguish between facts and opinions
> Keep it short and simple
> Explain why it's important
> State any major financial implications
> Say what should happen next

BREVITY

Winston Churchill once apologized for writing a long letter because 'I didn't have time to write a short one.' Brevity is not only the soul of wit, it is also another foundation stone of perfect communications.

If you are having trouble being brief, check whether:

- You are crystal clear about your essential message
- Sure of your audience
- Need more time and practice

The simplest brevity rule is keep your sentences and paragraphs short, choosing short words too. Pay particular attention to opening paragraphs which are key attention-getters.

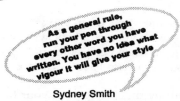

As a general rule, run your pen through every other word you have written. You have no idea what vigour it will give your style

Sydney Smith

When you have a first version of your communication you can usually cut it by half. Most management reports, for example, are too long, excessively packed with examples, repetitious and over explanatory.

BLOCK BUSTING

You know your subject well. You want to be succinct. You sit down facing a blank page or screen and . . .

. . . two hours later you are no further on. You are still wrestling with the opening sentence, the first paragraph or whatever. Why?

When you hit a block you could be:

- Unsure about what to say
- Lacking belief in what you have to say
- Needing more research
- Being dishonest with yourself

Test for the first of these by doing the 100-word condensing task mentioned above.

Test for the second by summarizing the core of your message into a single sentence which begins:

'What matters most to me personally is . . .'

Until you can 'feel' right inside about what you are saying it will not be easy to express your thoughts clearly in written form.

Test for inadequate research by listing quickly, on half a page, only the bare facts. If you cannot do it within say three minutes, you are either missing information or have not yet mastered your brief.

The hardest to uncover is when you are not being completely honest with yourself about what you are writing. It can happen when you feel strongly in some negative way about what you have to say.

Openly admitting these feelings in your first draft can help. For example, you might write: 'I feel really angry about this because . . .' This can miraculously release the blockage, letting words and ideas flow freely. If you wish, remove your 'admission' later.

The last tip for dealing with blocks is:

DON'T
GET IT
RIGHT
GET IT
WRITTEN

Write a first draft, however bad, inadequate, short or long. Once you have that first version, you have something to work with, to worry at and improve.

SUMMARIZE

The more you write the greater the need for summarizing. Outstanding management reports, for instance, nearly always hit you immediately with a brief, powerful synopsis.

After investing great effort in writing something it's

tiresome, even depressing trying to condense it into a couple of paragraphs or a single page. But that is what busy report readers want and expect.

Assume your reader will only have time to grab the summary and ignore the rest. That happens in many organizations. If you are a researcher, technical adviser, or specialist you may keep qualifying, giving the background, providing details. Try putting the entire material into an Appendix. Then work backwards, only taking material into the now empty body of the document if it meets the test:

'My reader MUST know this'

'Must know' material is distinctly different from information which is useful or interesting.

PRESENTATION QUALITY
When you have the final version of your document don't forget:

US Army Material Command

Why undermine good writing with bad spelling, poor grammar, or missed typos? Watch the details and be as professional as possible.

There is now no excuse for poor spelling since so many people have access to rapid spelling checkers on a word processor. There are also some inexpensive computer aids to 'Plain English Writing' such as Stylewriter, which identify a whole range of problems.

Complex words; jargon; over-used words; clichés;

tautologies; over writing; sexist writing; passive verbs; confused words and so on.

(For a free demonstration disk of Stylewriter contact the authors of *Perfect Communications* – see page v.)

You don't need a computer though, to follow the basic guidelines of readability, some of which we have already mentioned. Vary sentence and paragraph length to give your writing interest. Sentences of more than 20 to 25 words for instance, can be difficult to follow. Paragraphs with more than 14 to 20 lines can be overpowering.

Ask a colleague or friend to read your draft and identify areas that are unclear or not working well.

Finally, spare time to make your written communication look good. If it's a management report have it bound attractively. A well-presented document grabs more than its fair share of attention.

SUPPLY FACTS

Have enough factual evidence to support your:

> Analysis
> Conclusions
> Decisions
> Recommendations

Will the evidence stand up to scrutiny? If in doubt, say so.

Facts are an essential part of most communications and even selecting them is a personal affair. So:

- Choose relevant facts
- Distinguish between facts and assertion

- Explain any value judgments and preferences underlying your arguments
- Support facts with extra material and examples – if necessary relegated to appendices

Most management reports suffer from too many facts rather than too few. What matters is choosing the relevant ones. Also, report recipients appreciate it when you signal the switch from giving information to interpreting it.

MAKE NUMBERS COMPARATIVE

Many forms of written communication contain numbers. How can you make them effective?

First, always try to include comparisons. Few numbers make sense alone.

Example

To say 'this company made 50 patent applications last year' only becomes useful when placed in context such as: 'compared with 12 the previous year' or 'against the industry average of 25.'

Apart from avoiding too many figures, here are some basic ideas for making the best of those you include:

- Keep numbers simple, rounded where possible
- Check figures are reliable, accurate, understandable
- Give tables reference numbers and titles
- Include only a few numbers in a table so the pattern is apparent
- Reveal the pattern of any numbers, for example, by ranking them from highest to lowest
- Eliminate vertical lines between figures which prevent the eyes from easily reading across data
- If you number paragraphs keep your method simple – avoid systems with complicated subdivisions.

JARGON AND CLICHÉS

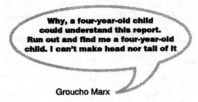

Why, a four-year-old child could understand this report. Run out and find me a four-year-old child. I can't make head nor tall of it

Groucho Marx

Jargon can be a form of aggression towards your audience. Even if your reader understands the jargon, it's no excuse. To communicate powerfully in writing keep jargon to a minimum.

How aware are you of using jargon? Write down here the 12 most common words in your particular specialist area:

_____ _____ _____

_____ _____ _____

_____ _____ _____

_____ _____ _____

Can you think of sensible alternatives?

Check for jargon by giving your written work to someone who does not know your field or subject matter. Or run your material through a computer system and watch as the jargon list mounts up, reducing your readability.

GRAPHICS
Good communicators know that a picture, chart or diagram can sometimes be more compelling than words.

Example

> *A company manager created a report and presented it to his senior management group. It was a straight piece of text, tables and recommendations. He finished with a simple drawing of a fallen Humpty Dumpty and the comment: 'If we ignore the facts here, this is what we'll get – and we won't be able to put it back together again!' For months afterwards, the group talked about 'The Humpty Dumpty effect'.*

Illustrations need to be well drawn, properly numbered, titled and look professional – especially in a management document. Each should give the reader a clear, specific message that only takes a moment to absorb.

Use graphs and charts only if they add a powerful new dimension to what you are saying. Otherwise they mystify rather than clarify.

Vary the sorts of graphics. For instance, a document with only pie charts may not necessarily be lively or compelling to read.

Written communication can be surprisingly visual. Ways to achieve variety include:

- changes of typeface
- changes of font
- listing within paragraphs
- numbering sections, paragraphs
- changing typeface colours
- cartoons, line-drawings, graphs, charts or photographs

It usually pays to double-space and leave decent margins. Number your pages and don't try to cram in too much. Be sparing in allowing paragraphs to run over to a new page.

GIVE CONCLUSIONS OR RECOMMENDATIONS

If what you are writing is a call to action, or even in-action, clarify what you want to happen. Don't expect your audience to guess.

Some people are reluctant to risk saying what should happen next, in case they are wrong or upset someone. If you avoid making recommendations or drawing conclusions in management documents you are doing only half your job.

Even without being asked, good communicators take the risk and pull the threads together to produce a coherent conclusion or set of recommendations. Conclusions need not be necessarily provocative or outrageous, they just need to be there.

BEING PERSUASIVE

During our course on Persuasive Writing, people often ask: 'how do I get people to agree to my proposals?' Apart from the quality of the writing, here are ten ways to increase your chances of gaining agreement:

- Ask for resources for a short period only
- Allow variations in how proposals would work
- Show how proposals could achieve what you claim
- Clarify why the proposal is an improvement
- Explain how your proposal is superior to others
- Justify costs
- Make proposals easy to understand
- Show how easy it would be to evaluate the outcome
- Show why the issue you are discussing is important
- Show how disastrous it will be without your idea

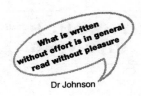

What is written
without effort is in general
read without pleasure

Dr Johnson

6

GETTING THROUGH: PERFECT PHONING

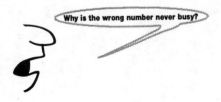

Why is the wrong number never busy?

You quickly recognize effective telephone users. They sound spontaneous, fresh and confident. They listen intently and get action.

When you use the phone well you enjoy it. It is an efficient use of your time and other people's. You regularly contact the right person and make a good first impression. Most of all you get results.

The phone is the first significant contact many customers have with a company. So it's an important image builder, and a powerful source of orders, enquiries and activity. It pays to improve telephone communications.

Your telephone communications consist of:

> You making calls
> People calling on you

You calling people means reviewing:

- Is this a good time for the person to talk?
- Does the person know who you are?
- Is it clear why you are calling?

- Is your message short and lucid?
- Is it the right person – for example a decision maker?
- What outcome do you want?
- Do they *hear* you smile?
- What is the agreed follow-up action?

People calling you means considering:

- How you answer the phone
- Why you answer the way you do
- Handling interruptions
- Message taking
- Dealing with pushy sales people
- The way you refer callers elsewhere
- Handling aggressive callers

Common to both situations is reviewing critically:

- The image you are portraying
- Your speed and clarity of speech
- Your skill at handling difficult callers
- The number of calls handled each day
- The type of calls
- Your busy periods
- People you speak to most
- New versus regular contacts
- The organization's rules for greeting callers
- Information you need, nearby
- Being assertive
- Listening skills

What these all amount to is a concern for:

- Building good relationships over the phone (see also Getting Acquainted)

Having the right attitude to handling calls is more important than worrying how your voice sounds and whether you should speak louder, softer, or add more variety and so on.

If you adopt the right approach from the start, focusing on building relationships, this is more likely to produce improvements than minor changes in how you speak.

How can you develop relationships when you are not physically present with someone? How do you make a disembodied voice feel valued, heard, and achieve what you want?

An essential requirement is:

- Know the purpose of the conversation

This may seem obvious, yet many phone calls are disasters because one or both parties are unsure what is the true purpose.

Example

A manager calls a junior colleague to ask a seemingly harmless question. Later in the conversation the real purpose emerges as a warning about some recent action.

A person rings offering you information or asking some inoffensive question. It turns out to be a disguised way of starting a hard sell.

Be aware of the realities of the phone as a communication medium:

- Intrusion: Some people resent even the brief loss of control over their lives when answering the phone
- Language: needs to be simple and uncomplicated as there is no immediate way to tell when the listener is frowning to show they are not following you.
- Excessive intimacy: you invade someone's ear; any closer and you'd risk a charge of assault

- Voice power: the voice is a great reflector – internal feelings quickly communicate, regardless of distance
- Distraction: doodling, riffling papers, typing, are all possible while talking; however, it quickly communicates when you are not fully attentive
- Speed: the rapid nature of the phone can wrongly suggest issues have been fully resolved
- Energy: it requires extra effort to make a conversation between two voices succeed
- Body language: there is none
- Cost: cumulatively the cost of calls is high

The telephone is a good way to talk to people without having to offer them a drink

Fran Lebowitz

The basics of perfect telephone communications are:

- Authenticity
- Clarity of message
- Listening
- Spontaneity
- Staying fresh
- An emphasis on action
- Specific telephone techniques

If you think of phone communications mainly in terms of building relationships it gives an important perspective to the basics. For example:

- Being yourself and conveying authenticity are essential because even the smallest sign of you being false, insincere or reading a script for instance, can be damaging.

This very often occurs when people have limited scope to greet callers in their own way or when tele-sales workers use a set formula which soon wears out its freshness (see below)

- You have only a limited time in which to get your message across before the other person suffers phone fatigue; condense your message down to answer in one sentence:

  'The reason I'm calling you is . . .'

- What does the other person need from you? It might be reassurance, hard facts, instructions, en-couragement. When you take care how to talk to the receiver he or she feels valued and wants to talk to you

- Active listening means giving verbal signs you are hearing and understanding

  This means offering more than grunts, mumbles and miscellaneous 'mms'. Offer short words to show you hear, understand, or agree with what they are saying

- Be willing not to dominate: instead listen carefully for any hidden messages behind the words – the subtext

- The phone creates unpredictable situations; re-sponding means adaptability, inventiveness and a willingness to take certain risks in handling the call imaginatively; if you work with a script make sure you keep varying it as you go along, which keeps you fresh and more spontaneous

- Sounding alert and energized is important and hard when phone work is repetitive, boring or both; find ways to vary the words, your style of talking and tone of voice to keep sounding fresh and interesting

- Focus on getting action through your phone communications; apart from social contacts few calls at work are simply to chat; use the phone purposefully to get what you want.

When you have a focus on action you tend to make sure you are speaking to the right person. For instance you may say directly: 'I'd like to speak to the person who chooses your photocopiers, are you the person I should be talking to?'

Specific phone techniques include:

- Grabbers: people don't give you long on the phone so have an opener to hold their attention
- Smiles: try smiling down the phone; it lifts your cheek muscles and improves your tone of voice
- Imagine: mentally picture the other person, even perhaps close your eyes to focus on them more clearly – they will detect your concentration and attention
- Transferring:

  - Be responsible for ensuring a suitable person is available before transferring calls
  - Take the caller's name and number
  - Tell the new receiver who is calling and something of the issue to save the original caller from having to repeat their story
  - Give the caller the name, position or section of the person to whom you are transferring them
  - Transfer the call and let the caller know what you are doing

- Holding: when you put someone on hold explain:

    - Whether the call goes through automatically
    - What shows the call is still connected, whether there is music, a tone or just silence
    - You will return within an agreed time
    - What to do if nothing happens

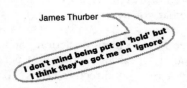

James Thurber

I don't mind being put on 'hold' but I think they've got me on 'ignore'

- Find ways to be helpful, rather than unhelpful; try thinking 'how can I help you' and your intent should shine through
- Answer every call quickly, within two or three rings
- Always return calls
- When making a series of planned calls keep a careful log to avoid calling the same person twice by mistake
- Avoid phones which let you speak hands free – they usually make you sound as if you are in a tin box; car phones are, for safety reasons, the exception
- If calling from a car phone volunteer your location
- The phone makes quick endings sound excessively abrupt so take time to handle the close pleasantly, as if you were shaking the person's hand
- Hold the phone so that you speak straight into the mouthpiece; some people dangle it under their chins and then wonder why the listener can't hear them
- Check back with the caller on important

information before finishing; repeat exactly any
telephone numbers, addresses or product details
- Take messages on a proper pad and have a way of
ensuring it is always replaced with another when
used up

While I was out did anyone take any messages?

No sir, are there any missing?

- With rude or aggressive callers:

  - Stay calm
  - Repeat what the caller said rather than ask
    them to re-state anything
  - Be polite
  - Show you will do all you can to resolve the
    problem
  - Apologize for mistakes and get the person's
    mind off what went wrong and on to what
    the caller wants done

Exercise

Listen to other people making a call and try to
decide what they are doing well or badly

Review your telephone layout:

Is the phone on your correct side?
Are pad and pen handy?
Is there enough space for writing messages?
Are frequently used phone numbers handy?
Can you use all the machine's facilities, like
call transfer, conferencing, call waiting sign
and so on?

Answering machines

You have reached the - family. What you hear is the barking of our killer Dobermann pinscher, Wolf.

Please leave a message after the tone

Answering message
in California, quoted
in Life, 1984

Make the outgoing message:

● short
● clear
● friendly
● convey energy

These invite the person to leave a message when otherwise they might ring off.

The unfriendliness of any outgoing announcement reflects on you, so try to make yours lively. Some people resort to creative ideas such as giving the message in the imitated voice of someone famous, using music, or saying something witty.

Whatever you invent make it brief. The other person is paying for the call. They may also be in a phone-box and running out of money while your creative message babbles on.

On your outgoing message ask the caller to say when

they rang and possibly the date. If there's a long pause before the message bleep, say so.

Ring yourself up and see how you sound. Change the message occasionally as regular callers become tired of the same one. Also each time you do so can inject new energy and purpose into it.

Every aspect of your telephone communication, from the message on the machine to how it's handled, counts in the communication process. It's not just when you are personally on the phone that you are giving a message – everything expresses who you are and your intention.

If the 'subtext' of the message isn't 'I really want to talk to you and want you to leave a message', then it's 'I don't want to talk to you, so don't leave a message, I'm not interested in human beings.'

If you have to speak to a machine:

> Keep your message brief and clear
> Say the time and date
> Repeat numbers, slowly
> Sign off positively
> If necessary ring back, having prepared a prompt note for yourself

7

GETTING TO THE MASSES: PERFECT MEDIA HANDLING

You cannot hope
to bribe or twist,
thank God! the
British journalist.
But, seeing what
the man will do
unbribed, there's
no occasion to.

Humbert Wolfe

A journalist from a tabloid paper telephones you just before lunch: 'Have you heard what's going on? What do you have to say? Do you deny it? Can you give an immediate comment?'

Good communicators handle these situations confidently, dealing with the press and other media contacts.

Media people sense a self-confident communicator. They receive a clear undefensive message. They hear the 'headline' from the communicator.

● Convert your message into a single headline phrase

Journalists are acutely aware of even slightly evasive behaviour. Not calling them back quickly for example, sends a loud and unhelpful message.

The Benefits
Even when someone is making an approach to you, take the initiative. By taking charge you refuse to become a victim.

With good media skills you get your message across

convincingly. You are also a source for information, comment, and advice. Instead of the media being a threat it becomes your ally.

Through mastering basic media skills you protect yourself and your organization.

We have helped managers in many companies to improve their media skills. A common belief we have found is that one can be evasive, defensive, aggressive or even lie, yet still come out on top. In our experience this seldom works in practice.

THE PRESS

You can say something in a certain spirit, with a smile, but when it appears in print, there's no smile

Marlon Brando

Be available

Be accessible to the press. Saying nothing will not necessarily avoid blunders, prevent misquotes or stop either you or your organization looking bad.

Using work or important meetings to refuse contact suggests you have something to hide.

Being available means you:

- ring back if you cannot deal with the journalist immediately
- explain clearly you are happy to talk, if necessary offering a specific time
- pass the person on responsibly; if the journalist

would be better talking to someone else in the company check they are available to deal with the call
- say when you cannot give a formal comment and then stick to this, if necessary calmly repeating it

Discover the context

At the start of each media contact discover the context:

- Is the publication national, local or specialist?
- What's the issue and why is it hot?
- Who else have they contacted?
- Where will the story appear – in a special feature, a particular column and what is the person's deadline?
- Why do they want to speak to you or your company?
- Is the journalist freelance or employed by a particular publication and if so which one?
- Is this a speculative piece of research or is there a definite story commitment?

Respect deadlines

All journalists work to deadlines, often more unyielding than ones faced by managers. Respect these pressures and work within their time constraints.

However, never let deadlines intimidate you. You can often turn them to your advantage by explaining you cannot supply the information needed in that timescale. Surprisingly, the 'deadline' may miraculously extend a few more hours, days or even weeks.

You know more

However knowledgeable the press person appears, you know more about your job and company. You talk from a position of strength.

- Avoid drifting into unknown territory

- Stick to what you know
- Offer only facts you can verify or be sure about

You can choose whether or not to speak. It's a journalist's skill to encourage you to talk but perfect communicators do so on their own terms.

Avoid bluffing; find an honest way of saying you can't or won't respond.

Anticipate

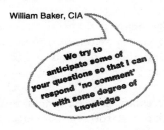

William Baker, CIA

We try to anticipate some of your questions so that I can respond 'no comment' with some degree of knowledge

Try guessing in advance what questions you might face. What are your likely answers?

- Discover what concerns the journalist
- Identify tough questions and possible answers
- Discuss your approach with an experienced person
- Prepare interesting new information to offer
- Develop quotable quotes

Find an angle

Journalists want an angle or slant to make their article interesting. Ask yourself:

- What's the headline?
- What are the three main points I want made in an article?
- How can I strengthen my message?

Quotable quotes

Interesting quotes are the core of many articles. Quotable quotes tend to be some of these:

Short	Insightful
Clear	Critical
Relevant	Challenging
Dramatic	Provocative
Funny	Newsworthy

AND ABOVE ALL USABLE

Use examples, or 'for instances' and describe interesting events involving real people.

Admit ignorance

Bluffing your way out of trouble is usually a mistake. Journalists are good at detecting such behaviour.

- If necessary, request time to discover the facts
- Stick to the truth, you are less likely to contradict yourself

Respect competitors

Avoid detrimental remarks about named competitors. A skilled journalist can use such remarks to get the other party to make equally unpleasant comments. It looks as if you are having a public slanging match. The only winner is the publication.

Talk on your terms

You can exercise some control over interviews.

You may wish to talk 'off the record, and not for attribution' – which means that no source will be indicated. This is stronger than just 'off the record' which journalists may treat with varying degrees of respect.

Always state whether you are speaking on or off

the record. Clarify whether your company will be quoted by name, even if you are not. By insisting at the start on clear ground rules you gain both a real and a psychological advantage. After all, the journalist needs you.

No matter how friendly you become with a journalist:

● **Assume anything said might be quoted!**

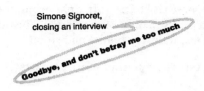

Simone Signoret,
closing an interview

Goodbye, and don't betray me too much

Be patient with ignorance
The lack of knowledge of some journalists can be stunning.

● Deal with all questions tolerantly and with good humour

Roll with the punches
Journalists working under pressure are sometimes aggressive, abrasive or rude. Never respond in kind.

● Use phrases like:

'That's one point of view, but I have another . . .'
'You could say that, I wouldn't agree though . . .'
'No I don't accept that, let me tell you

> why . . .'
>
> 'You may feel that, let me explain my view . . .'

- Let silence show disapproval for ill-mannered behaviour
- If something is offensive say so; suggest the journalist would find it more helpful to speak to someone else; then wait for the person to change tack.

Give leads

If you have little to say don't give a brush off. Instead suggest where else to try, offer phone numbers or contacts. Keep a list handy of professional institutes, trade associations, industry bodies and so on.

- Suggest where to find more contacts

Question for question

If you consider yourself good at asking the right questions use this skill with the media.

For example, if an interview becomes difficult try responding with questions of your own. You may not receive answers but it can change the pace of the interview, giving you a breathing space.

Build contacts

Journalists rely on some regular contacts whom they don't want to antagonize. Build relationships with people you feel you can trust:

- Take the initiative and contact selected journalists with interesting information, leads, gossip
- Spend time just chatting over a drink or a meal
- Show an interest in the person's own background – how long have they been a journalist; who else have they worked for; what other stories are they working on at present; what are their particular concerns and so on

One question leads to another

Answer one question and it's hard to avoid the next one. Make it clear when you are not going to be drawn, rather than offering a barrage of words. For example:

'Sorry, I've nothing to say about that' and continue saying this, pleasantly.

Know company ground rules

One of the greatest concerns of the managers we train is speaking out of line with company policy. Familiarize yourself with what your organization expects in dealing with the press. What are the requirements, the restrictions, the support, the policy line and so on?

Make it two-way

Enjoy your involvement with the press

● Turn the interview into a two-way conversation

You can learn plenty of helpful information from your contact if you do some digging too. No interview should be one-way.

Avoid waffle

Journalists want facts, information, views, opinions and quotes. As paid listeners they will encourage you to go on . . . and on.

Avoid talking just to fill the space

● Speak succinctly and then – full stop

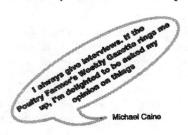

I always give interviews. If the Poultry Farmer's Weekly Gazette rings me up, I'm delighted to be asked my opinion on things

— Michael Caine

RADIO

Be yourself

- Use your personality, don't hide behind a script, or being a 'corporate spokesperson'
- Companies consist of people; you're entitled to be YOU
- Your personality gives a broadcast that special quality

Prepare

Prepare key points and practise them on a colleague, a tape recorder, or even the dog. If it's a 'chat show', be prepared to chat. If however, it's an interview:

- Use short sentences and phrases that come across immediately

People who ramble are seldom invited back.

Preparation also means checking whether the broadcast is live or recorded, and knowing company policy on issues about which you may be speaking.

Breathe

Tension easily transfers to the voice, sometimes raising the pitch to a whine creating endless 'ums' and 'ers',

- Before speaking breathe deeply several times, exhaling slowly

Continue regulating your breath during your broadcast to provide calmness and a sense of space.

Vary your voice

Give your voice plenty of up and down sounds to make it more interesting to hear. You'll do it naturally if you are talking with conviction, commitment and passion.

Visualize

Visualize the microphone as a real person, someone you know and like. Talk to it using smiles, nods and facial expressions. It may feel odd, but your 'aliveness' will communicate.

Pace

- Deliver your message with pace to avoid droning
- Inject new energy into each comment

Scrap scripts

With a script you risk becoming trapped into reading boring material, and paper rustling.

- Stick to key points on a single page or a card

If you make an official announcement type it large and in double spacing for easy reading.

Be friendly

Formal spokespeople very often sound stilted or defensive. Treat an interviewer as a friend, someone you enjoy meeting, not a Nosey Parker trying to embarrass you. Friendliness communicates to listeners.

Find what matters

You speak with more power and conviction when something matters to you. You will be more spontaneous, confident and compelling.

- Focus on what you most care about

Be early

Arrive early at the studio. It gives you time to unwind and absorb the atmosphere.

If speaking at your office, on the phone or at a special location, free yourself from other distractions at least five or ten minutes before you're due to talk.

Use the time to breathe deeply, relax and think about what you might say.

TV AND VIDEO

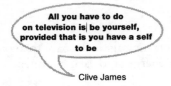

All you have to do on television is be yourself, provided that is you have a self to be

Clive James

The basic principle of 'write your own headline' applies just as much here too (see above).

It's visual
This is a visual medium, so non-verbal communication issues matter. Viewers absorb your message from all the signals you give, not just the words.

● Watch your body language

Appearance
Take care with your appearance. Does it convey the image you want?

● Choose appropriate clothes you feel good in
● Clothes with narrow lines or check patterns can cause the camera problems and be distracting
● Sit up straight, without slouching, yet relaxed
● Sit still – moving around looks fidgety. This does not mean staying transfixed and immobile; just avoid constantly twitching or making gestures which take you suddenly out of camera.

Breath
It can be intimidating being on TV or video, and even worse in a studio with its harsh lights, technicians and equipment.

● Try 'rethinking' what is happening:

>   'This is an interesting place to be, what can I learn?'

- Do regular relaxation exercises to help you stay calm
- Keep breathing steadily: a couple of deep breaths then some gentle steady breaths

Breathe well and you can handle almost anything.

Technical terrors
TV is a technical medium often needing considerable preparation to make it work well. You may have to sit around for ages till it's your moment.

Everywhere people are doing mysterious jobs: camera operators, make-up, lighting, sound. Hardly intelligible conversations are taking place around you.

- Stay focused on your purpose. Keep reminding yourself:

> 'I'm here because I want to . . .'
> 'What I most want to say is . . .'

During the waiting period some TV companies offer hospitality areas. A few drinks will *not* help you relax or perform better. Some famous film stars may survive appearing drunk on screen, but it won't help communicate your message.

The need is always to:

- Stay Alert

Be direct
Talk directly to the interviewer holding steady eye contact. Looking away even once can appear decidedly shifty.

If you are speaking directly to the camera for an internal

corporate message, a sales pitch or an appeal, imagine someone behind the lens – a particular person you know and like. Talk to them and avoid looking elsewhere.

Tone
If you are representing an organization make sure you hit the right tone.

A danger of being a 'company spokesperson' is the temptation to distance yourself and thus the organization from any emotional reaction.

Calmness is admirable, but not if it makes you seem inhuman or unfeeling.

- Stay in touch with your feelings

Rehearse
It's always useful to practise before facing the camera. Get somebody to interview you. If possible practise using your own video equipment.

If necessary get some help. We often work with managers, for example, who find they gain from rehearsing with professionals who can save time in getting the best from their media performance.

QUESTION TIME
Answering media questions can be either an exciting, rewarding experience or a daunting undertaking.

Handling questions well, for example on a panel, or during an interview demands various techniques:

Prepare
To prepare for something which may seem spontaneous the best way is:

- Think about the questions you may be asked

- Play devil's advocate: what's the worst question you could be asked and how might you handle it?

You're always on

Even when not answering you are communicating actively, using non–verbal signals:

- Stay sitting upright
- Appear ready to answer
- Focus on the person speaking
- Listen attentively, with eyes open

Talk to the audience

Speak straight to the audience as much as you can. Address the person asking the question, then open it out to everyone.

Beware of talking only to the questioner, chairperson or to other people on a panel.

No put downs

Remarks that scoff at or belittle your audience will do you harm, not them.

Even if you think the audience is ignorant or over simple, it's better to keep that opinion to yourself.

Subtext

Often a question is a statement, rather than an enquiry. Check it out.

If someone asks a question and seems worried by an unspoken matter, try expressing it for them.

For example:

> 'You seem to be suggesting . . .'
> 'I wonder if you are really saying . . .'

'What you seem to be implying is . . .'

Satisfied customer

A good question handler was Sit Peter Imbert the Metropolitan Police Commissioner. Faced with difficult or challenging questions he invariably restated them. This gave him time to frame the answer and made the questioner feel valued.

Respect your questioner by occasionally saying:

- 'Does that answer your question; have I covered the point?'

Energy

When on the receiving end of a series of questions it takes more energy than usual to communicate well.

A too relaxed or laid back approach may work for some media personalities but can easily fall flat when you try it. So stay

- Alert
- Involved
- Enthusiastic

PART THREE

What's the Point?

8

GETTING ACQUAINTED: PERFECT RELATIONSHIPS

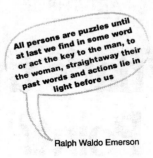

All persons are puzzles until at last we find in some word or act the key to the man, to the woman, straightaway their past words and actions lie in light before us

Ralph Waldo Emerson

WHY BOTHER?

Communicating so that you are understood is just a start. Being understood and understanding others isn't enough. Another essential ingredient of perfect communications is:

● Building relationships

This means you are involved with a whole network of people in which everyone understands one another and can take suitable action.

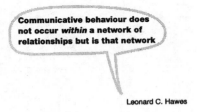

Communicative behaviour does not occur *within* a network of relationships but is that network

Leonard C. Hawes

Positive, productive relationships are easy to spot because people:

● get on with you and you with them

- enjoy being around you
- perform favours without expecting an immediate return
- trust you and you them
- willingly share information, contacts and other important sources

Productive relationships occur as you discover more about people. Not just their work roles or other surface information. You also know something of their personal lives, interests and hobbies, beliefs and opinions, what they value in life and care about.

Exercise

Try making a list of the following:

What I know or don't know about the people I work with
What I know or don't know about those I relate to regularly, for example customers
What these people know about me personally
What I appreciate and value about these people
When I have said I value them

Without answers to these sorts of questions you have limited scope to understand these people and therefore build links with them. It's time for some detective work.

Exercise

Use your curiosity.

Discover some personal details about your customers. We mean customers in the broadest sense – anyone you serve in some form. This needn't involve you in lengthy or nosey conversations. Just look for opportunities to communicate. For example, if the person has been on holiday try asking where they went and what it was like. Take a real, not superficial interest in the answers. When you show you are curious it can open a fruitful exchange of information.

The more you know, the more you expand your points of contact. You have more areas to which you can both relate, on which to build links.

Exercise

Find an opportunity to tell somebody what you value about them. See if you can slip it into the conversation. For example: 'I thought you'd be able to help me out, you're great at this sort of thing'; 'You seem to know a lot about this, I'd really value your opinion on . . .'

NETWORKING

Networking is when you build a pattern of relationships. If you like, it's your own database. While memorizing many details, good networkers also write down a great deal. They know it's impossible to remember all the details that oil the wheels of communication to build relationships. Some people use a fat address book, a personal organizer, even a card index. Some dedicated networkers even use a computer for cross-referencing, to trigger reminders to call people back and so on.

Exercise

Step 1.   Who do you know?

List all the contacts you have. Take your time to build the list up. You know more people than you think.

Record more than names and addresses. Note important projects, family details, likes and dislikes, skills and contacts.

Step 2.   Can you group these people?

See if these people fall into natural clusters. For example: a group you deal with regularly for business; a set of people to whom you speak rarely but who are loyal to you; a further set who do similar work but in a different industry.

Step 3. Answer the questions:

What do these people offer me now?

What else might they be able to offer me?

What can I offer them?

This is how networkers, consciously or not, build their database and develop their relationships.

Freelancers constantly use networks, but anyone can create and use one. You can do it within an organization and beyond it. When you need help or information it's time to 'mine' your network.

Networkers never worry about asking for help because they are keen to offer it in return. They know that what they put into the network governs what they can extract from it.

If you work for an organization here's a scary exercise:

Exercise

Imagine you now need to look for another job. It could be because it's time to move, the firm is closing, you become redundant or are suddenly sacked.

Make a list of at least 25 people you will call to help you:

hunt for a new employer
create a new job for yourself

When was the last time you called each of these people? What have you done for each of them in the last 12 months?

When you have a working network one person refers you to another, or knows about a source to help you. Keen networkers say that to communicate a personal message or send a precious parcel to someone anywhere in the world all you need is seven people in a room. Somebody will know someone who knows someone who . . .

When you invest time and energy in people, you show you care – and they don't forget it. Keep up your contacts. You can hardly ask a favour when you haven't spoken to someone for five years.

Ways of keeping in touch include:

- FAVOURS: whenever possible do favours for people; send copies of articles you know will interest them; recommend films; places or events you think they'd enjoy; keep them in mind when job vacancies occur. It's a question of tuning in – focusing on what they may need instead of waiting for them to ask.

- CARDS: send Christmas cards, congratulation cards, postcards, any cards. America's most successful car sales agent kept a list of all his customers' birthdays and anniversaries, children and interests, and regularly sent personalized cards to each client. Pick something which expresses who you are or what you are about.

- THANK YOUs: if people do you a favour, grab the opportunity to thank them with some chocolates, a bottle of wine or a suitable gift.

- SOCIAL: go for a drink or a coffee with someone, so you can develop the relationship; spare time for them and they'll find time for you – when you need it.
- PARTIES: these can develop your network at an express speed. Create each event around a core of people with similar interests and include on the lists people you know only slightly – clients, suppliers, neighbours, guests met at friends' parties and so on. Ensure every guest meets at least two people who could be useful or interesting for them to know.

- CREATIVE FAXES: design some amusing faxes to cheer people up on a bad day.

- OUTINGS: arrange a social outing and invite your contacts; one successful communicator we know regularly takes his contacts down the Thames on his cabin cruiser. You don't need your own boat however to get the same results.

HELPING OTHERS TO TALK

Communications must be two-way if positive relationships are to develop. That means getting them and then keeping them talking. How do you do that?

GETTING THEM TALKING

- PERMISSION: give people the go ahead to talk; it can be important, especially if your work or social standing could get in the way. Phrases like: 'Tell me about . . .'; 'I'd like to hear . . .'; What do you think about . . .' signal to someone it's all right to start speaking. Fatal accidents have occurred because junior crew members who tried to bring problems to their superiors' attention were discouraged from speaking.

- QUESTIONS: ask open-ended questions – who,

how, what, where, why, when. These encourage people to elaborate rather than give one-word answers.

- SENSITIVE AREAS: watch out for what *isn't* said; if you know something is going on and the other person seems unable to talk about it, they may be waiting for you to raise it.

KEEPING THEM TALKING

- FEED THEM: do this with slight nods, smiles or sounds ('mmm', 'yes') or short encouraging phrases such as 'Go on', 'I see'.

- SILENCES: if someone says something especially difficult or important do not reply the moment they finish. Instead leave a little gap. Show you are absorbing what they have said. A short silence sometimes prompts a person to say a final few words – which may be highly relevant.

- MIRRORING: repeat aloud feelings or concerns the other person has shared. For example, 'I can see you're worried about . . .' 'Sounds like you're really angry . . .'.

- KEY WORDS: ask the meaning of a key word or phrase.

- BUILD: take what people say and build on it, rather than always starting on a new line of your own.

- CHECK UNDERSTANDING: regularly check whether you understand correctly the other person's message.

Balanced conversations create communication where

- both sides listen about equally
- the amount each person says is about equal

Exercise

Try analysing your next three conversations.

Having finished a conversation, review:

What happened?
Who spoke most?
Were there periods of silence?
Was space left for people, including you, to contribute?
Was there space to express thoughts and feelings?
How could you have made the exchange more equal?
Who interrupted whom and how often?
When talking to people did you look directly at them?
Were you always talking as if in a hurry?
Could you readily summarize what the other person said?
What could you do differently next time?

Try asking a trusted friend or colleague to discuss these with you.

To build good relationships helpful listening is essential. This is not the same as keeping quiet while someone else speaks. To listen well, you:

- **L**eave space and time to hear
- **I**nterrupt only at the risk of killing the conversation
- **S**eek not to judge but to understand
- **T**arget your whole attention on the speaker
- **E**ncourage them and listen even if you disagree
- **N**ever frame a response while they are speaking

Exercise

Your mind keeps wandering while a speaker is in full flood. Instead of looking around bored, fidgeting or trying to interrupt, you continue to look at them while saying to yourself some or all of these:

'This is their time'
'What can I hear behind the words?'
'What does this person want most?'

GETTING CLOSER

Communication becomes deeper and more intimate when people exchange sensitive information about themselves. This is called 'self-disclosure' and when it occurs gradually, it builds two-way trust.

- BE SELECTIVE: indiscriminate self-disclosure, like trying to be friends with everyone, does not encourage trust or good communication
- SHOW INTEREST: take an interest in others and they'll probably start taking an interest in you
- USE SENSITIVITY: handle the information you receive carefully; it's hard to establish trust when people fear what they say will be handled badly

IN SUMMARY

Building relationships through effective communication happens in four broad stages:

- Decide what you really feel and want (see GETTING REAL)
- Explain so the other person understands (see GETTING TO THE POINT)
- Encourage the other person to do the same
- Find workable arrangements with one another

Ann Morrow Lindbergh

Good communication is as stimulating as black coffee, and just as hard to sleep after

9

GETTING PEACE: PERFECT CONFLICT RESOLUTION

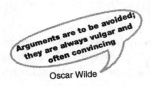

Arguments are to be avoided; they are always vulgar and often convincing

Oscar Wilde

In every communication there is scope for conflict. Perfect communicators are able to:

- Anticipate it
- Prepare for it
- Deal with it

When you handle conflicts well, they come to the surface for resolution. All parties feel heard and a course of action is agreed which is acceptable to everyone involved. The conflicts are dealt with speedily and resolved without undue rancour or violence.

Conflict often exists whether you like it or not, and is often unavoidable. It may indeed be healthy and creative – without it some situations might never alter.

Jeremy Rifkind, US
Economist

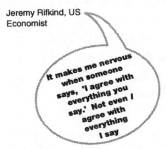

It makes me nervous when someone says, 'I agree with everything you say.' Not even I agree with everything I say

Many people prefer to avoid confronting virtually any conflict because:

- It can produce anxiety
- People may complain or quit
- They fear it won't do any good
- They don't know how to manage it successfully
- It might make things worse than they are now

Conflicts are often 'messy', and there's rarely a simple answer. No matter how much we may want to deal with them in a sensible and rational way, they often remain uncontrollable and insoluble. So, often we suppress them and 'hope they'll go away'.

Although it may be necessary to suppress seriously destructive or violent conflict, most conflicts need to be dealt with. Avoiding them wastes people's time and energy. In organizations it may also waste capital assets, damage relationships with customers and ultimately, therefore, profits. Confronting conflict is usually sensible because:

- Avoiding the problem won't make it go away
- The problem will probably get worse, not better
- Other problems may afterwards be easier to resolve
- People may afterwards be more productive and happier

Therefore, perfect communicators excel at handling rather than always preventing it. To deal with it:

- **You listen**

    See it from the other person's view
    Feel the other's emotional state
    Avoid discounting the other's message
    Collect all possible information

Roy West, Principal,
Mosby Middle School,
Richmond, Virginia

If you're going
to be a bridge,
you've got to be
prepared to be
walked on

● **You show respect**

For the dignity of all stakeholders
Honour people's feelings
Accept the other party has genuine concerns
Say nothing demeaning
Focus on issues and behaviour, not personalities

● **You assert**

Say what you mean
Explain what you want
Express how you feel
Avoid aggression

● **You understand**

The issues
Who is involved
What the other party says
What the other party means
Why the other party feels this way
What the other party wants

● **You seek**

The facts
Distinctions between matters of principle and opinion

Solutions, not necessarily always compromise
Evidence to show conflict is resolved

Conflict can arise between individuals, groups and within or beyond an organization. Each may need different approaches for a resolution.

It helps to use a methodical approach and various strategies. Equally important is staying light on your feet and remaining willing to see what the situation requires.

Where possible try following this structured approach:

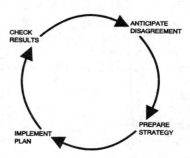

ANTICIPATION

- What are the issues; seek feedback; collect facts; analyse how events may develop
- Who are stakeholders; discover opinions
- What are the causes: strong feelings; divergent goals; missing or wrong information; inappropriate methods

PREPARE STRATEGY

- Adopt a broad strategy: flexible, willing to alter stance to some degree; or inflexible, unwilling to alter position to any great extent

- Choose a style which suits the occasion:

Bargaining
- define what both parties want
- identify minimum demands for resolution
- state common advantages of different choices
- encourage offers and counter offers
- establish time when bargaining must finish

Unilateral decision
- describe your position very clearly
- show conviction
- don't be evasive

Joint problem solving
- agree a joint view of the task
- avoid selecting a solution too early
- share views and issues
- listen without being defensive
- seek alternatives which satisfy all interests

Create rules for making decisions
- identify the choice of methods
- gain agreement on how to make choices, such as voting, consensus, by committee
- obtain support for whatever results occur
- handle further conflict using the rules

Smoothing over differences

- ensure everyone has the same information
- stress what people already agree about
- play down importance of differences

People need a chance to see how much agreement is possible between seemingly intractable opponents

Robert Redford,
Actor

Be willing to mix and match strategies and styles. In particular avoid being rigid, aloof, or indecisive.

IMPLEMENT PLAN

- Recognize and respond to feelings
- Use chosen strategy and tactics
- Spot and break potential deadlocks by:

    adjournments; bargaining; decision rules such as voting; standoffs; setting an issue to one side and so on

- Keep this process moving

CHECK RESULTS

- Assess what has happened
- Identify the need for any more action
- Start further action

Resolving conflict need not be a win or lose situation. Perfect communicators usually try to make everyone win by:

- Knowing their own mind and their 'bottom line'
- Understanding the power situation

- Gaining goodwill for solutions, using rapport and communication skills
- Wanting resolutions
- Creating solutions that allow all parties to start afresh, feeling uncompromised.

Remember, disagreements are natural and useful. Part of a developing relationship is acknowledging the separateness and individuality of the other person.

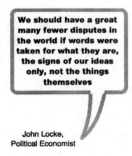

We should have a great many fewer disputes in the world if words were taken for what they are, the signs of our ideas only, not the things themselves

John Locke,
Political Economist

Rows

Rows though, are breakdowns in communication. The word or event triggering them is seldom the real issue. A row is rarely about what it seems to be about. So what else is going on? If it's not about the missed meetings, dirty cups or poorly presented document, what is it about?

Usually there's an underlying build-up of anger, disappointment, or concern about losing one's personal power in some way.

When locked into an ongoing feud with someone you are obviously not going to communicate effectively. And no matter how much we would like to, we can rarely change the other person. All you can do is work on your 50 per cent of the relationship. So how do you start changing the situation inside you? Firstly it's worth noting that your reaction to the other person is often prompted because he or she triggers unhappy memories, relating to one's own personal or family history.

Exercise

Try keeping a diary of your angry moments. Note incidents triggering them and add below what else you were feeling at the time: sadness, fear, guilt, envy, jealousy, insecurity, hurt pride, self dislike and so on.

Review: 'when have I felt these emotions before?' This allows you to realize it's not just about the other person, and keeps things in perspective.

Another well tried method is called 'releasing'. Suppose you are locked into feeling extremely angry with your manager. You obviously won't communicate well in that state yet just cannot seem to forgive him for his actions. You feel trapped in your emotional reaction and can't think how you can ever get out of it.

A useful releasing device is the One Per Cent Solution. You locate a powerful feeling which could be stopping communication and think or say aloud:

'Could I let go of **only one per cent** of wanting to change (that situation)?'

Letting go of one per cent of the wanting is often much easier than letting go of all of it.

If you can let go at all . . . at least you know you *can* let go

Finally, a constructive tactic known to produce results where two or more parties are in conflict is the 'Describe My Position' method:

1. John disagrees with Mary.

2. They decide to use the 'Describe my position' method.

3. John briefly explains his position; Mary says nothing, merely listens.

4. Mary now re-states John's position. She must obtain his agreement that she has correctly understood and described his position without necessarily agreeing with it.

   If required, John explains how Mary's description of his position is still not yet accurate. John must help Mary correctly state his position, not just sit back and let her struggle. Until he is fully satisfied she must keep trying to describe his position correctly.

5. It is now Mary's turn to state her position. John also listens without interruption. Then he re-states Mary's position until she confirms it's an accurate description of where she stands.

6. Both parties now try to explain precisely where they differed and how to resolve these differences.

7. Using any differences remaining, the whole process starts again until there is a resolution.

This method assumes both John and Mary are willing to work at dealing with the conflict. Nothing will work if either party is still out to 'get' the other person. Revenge may be sweet, but it will never produce peace. While the above method can sometimes be heavy going, it does rapidly remove the heat from many conflict situations, forcing both sides to focus on communicating well.

The focus is firmly on listening, which promotes a good understanding about the real areas of difference and so how to deal with them.

Try it!

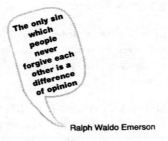

The only sin which people never forgive each other is a difference of opinion

Ralph Waldo Emerson

10

GETTING BETTER: PERFECT FEEDBACK

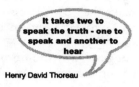

It takes two to speak the truth - one to speak and another to hear

Henry David Thoreau

Perfect feedback is communication at its best. It is giving and receiving both praise and criticism. It helps develop relationships. It supports people to improve and grow. And in organizations, it gets action.

Feedback helps people to do their jobs properly – to understand what's going on, feel involved, ask questions and so on. It helps avoid mistakes and to plan work more effectively.

During the feedback process, giver and receiver share feelings and sometimes personal information. Good feedback is therefore often an intimate exchange.

Feedback reinforces what you want to happen. For example, when a meeting ends you may suggest: 'Let's recap – what action have we agreed to take?' This type of feedback is summarizing (see also GETTING TO THE POINT).

CHARACTERISTICS OF PERFECT FEEDBACK
You can recognize perfect feedback. It is:

- wanted – not imposed
- helpful – discovering what should be done, not telling them what to do

- timely – given without delay; in a suitable place; at a suitable time; not rushed
- relevant – what the receiver needs
- descriptive – not evaluative; observations given without judging them as good and bad; individuals are free to make their own assessment
- specific – sticks to facts and incidents, avoiding generalities
- practical – suggests how to improve in areas over which the person has some control

GIVE OR GET?
Feedback is either a gift to people: **FEED** them.
Or it can be said to get people: stab in the **BACK**.

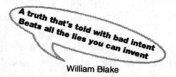

A truth that's told with bad intent
Beats all the lies you can invent

William Blake

Feedback consists of praise, criticism – or a mixture of both. Unselective or dishonest praise is neither helpful nor useful.

Positive feedback is a GIVE – a stroke which recognizes both person and performance. It nourishes – helps us develop and do our work well.

Destructive feedback puts people down or makes them feel bad about themselves and is a GET. It's mental back-stabbing which equates to 'I'll get you', and is useless. People meeting a GET usually give up, reject criticism or counter-attack.

Like any giving, perfect feedback has spin-offs. It encourages further feedback and creates trust. When you offer useful feedback you gain credibility and people take your communications seriously.

Harry S. Truman

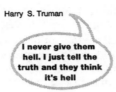

I never give them hell. I just tell the truth and they think it's hell

WHOSE AGENDA?

Poor feedback which is a GET never serves the receiver. When you are *giving* feedback, keep checking it is useful and is not part of some secret purpose of your own. For example, if you are telling someone about their faults or weaknesses, and you'd been longing to do it for some time, will your feedback help or hinder if you approach it that way?

If you catch yourself speaking or thinking any phrase listed below, check whether you can express it more helpfully:

- you should have known better
- I can see no point in
- you must realize
- I find it difficult to believe
- with respect
- that's irrelevant
- don't be stupid
- that's good but . . .

SCENE SETTING

Do not use a hatchet to remove a fly from your friend's forehead

Chinese Proverb

Perfect feedback respects the other person and his or her

organization. When planning to give it, never rush the receiver or take them by surprise. In a positive and friendly tone tell them you need a meeting, or time to talk honestly, and explain its purpose.

If possible give people a choice of receiving feedback by offering

>When to receive it

>From whom

>In what form

Encourage people to ask for it rather than imposing it on them. It's more useful that way.

To what extent is the receiver happy to receive feedback? How would he or she prefer it – written, spoken, in private or with a someone else there, as support?

It is fine to speak about your feelings; rather than just give facts, just be honest about them. Say you are going to talk about how you feel about the situation.

Avoid 'fuzzies' such as

>'You should take more pride in your work'
>'I want you to adopt a more professional approach'
>'You need to work on being more decisive'
>'You're going to have to improve your attitude'

These are too general to describe how you want the person to behave. They are abstractions or fuzzies. They sound good but they are not useful because they don't say what the person needs to do to perform better.

To avoid fuzzies, use action words rather than abstractions. Action words provide specific feedback about specific behaviour you want to see.

Exercise

Name three 'fuzzies' you have either used yourself or heard used at work. Transform them by using specific, practical ideas.

BEING TACTFUL

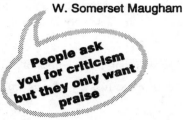

W. Somerset Maugham

People ask you for criticism but they only want praise

No one likes criticism. It hurts, so take that into account. If giving painful feedback which you believe is 'for someone's own good' be tactful, not just truthful. With tact, people will often accept criticism as helpful.

Be vulnerable and perhaps start by volunteering some self-criticism. Ask open questions that begin with HOW, WHEN, WHERE, WHY, WHO, WHAT and discuss facts without offering judgments yourself.

While criticisms are often best sandwiched between two positive pieces of information, don't follow this slavishly – it can seem obvious and even absurd. Rather admit you are going to make critical comments and do so tactfully:

- go for the ball, not the player
- be personal – acknowledge it's your opinion
- use only first-hand knowledge
- explain the effect of mistakes
- focus discussion on desired improvements
- do not blame or punish
- restrict yourself to what's under discussion
- don't revive old mistakes

Exercise

You are planning to give feedback on a specific issue in the future. Apply the above check-list to the proposed feedback; tick off each suggestion as you incorporate it in your notes.

One element of tact is avoiding emotionally loaded expressions which cause people to feel resentful, hurt or angry:

- Criticisms that include possibly insulting words

    - you're too fussy; that was stupid; for God's sake . . .

- Questions putting people on the defensive

    - is that the best you can do? d'you expect me to believe a story like that?

- Extreme statements or exaggerations

    - that was the most ridiculous action imaginable; you always blame other people ·

SIGNS TO WATCH FOR

You can tell when you've used one of these forms of feedback or a fuzzie because the other person stops being receptive and instead may:

Appear confused
Start to argue
Show an expression of disagreement
Shake head back and forth
Seem startled or astonished
Furrow eyebrows
Raise eyes to ceiling
Begin to interrupt
Fold arms firmly
Lean back in the chair
Look anxious to speak

USING HUMOUR

Humour which arises spontaneously from feedback can help people relax by breaking the tension and encouraging a mood of goodwill. It is a valuable tool.

Planned jokes, though, seldom work. Humour can too easily become a Get, so be careful to avoid using it this way.

SILENCE

Silence is another useful way of helping people to accept information about themselves or their organization. If they reject what you say and become defensive – talking quickly, justifying and so on – simply stay silent. Don't feed their defences by murmuring 'mm' or 'yes'.

Use the silence to examine your own feelings and needs. Are you angry? Are you afraid? Do you want to pursue the subject? Silence can give people pause for thought, time to listen to their own voice and take stock of what they are saying. Gradually they become silent themselves.

If the receiver has been full of excuses and apologies, use the silence to change these by asking 'what can you do to overcome these problems?' Or ask 'do you know what the problem is?' Listen to the analysis and see if you can convert it to a solution.

FEEDBACK TO YOU

Perfect communicators are good at receiving feedback too. If what you hear is a GIVE you can relax and learn from it. It it's a GET then:

- either declare the tone of the feedback is unacceptable and suggest you will welcome an exchange another time
- or sit quietly, breathe regularly, and try to hear whether anything at all is of value to you.

As a receiver you can encourage helpful feedback. Invite it about a specific piece of work. Reassure the person you don't take exception to criticism. Show you are keen to receive information to help you improve your performance.

When you receive feedback well, you are curious. You listen calmly and actively and respond assertively:

- ask for elaboration if you don't understand
- keep calm – don't be hostile or aggressive
- concentrate on what both of you are feeling
- keep what is said in perspective

Watch for unspoken feedback. You can learn much from body language, tone of voice, facial gestures and from what people do. If there are contradictions between what the receiver says and how they behave, explore the subject until they volunteer any reservations. Do not accept comforting words while failing to hear the real message.

BLOCKING FEEDBACK

He that won't be counselled can't be helped

Benjamin Franklin

You are rejecting useful feedback if you:

- 'tune out' from what is said
- repeatedly interrupt
- answer sarcastically
- make personal attacks on the speaker ('the trouble with you is . . . ')
- quibble over minor facts
- justify yourself: 'yes but . . .' 'I only . . .' 'the point

is . . .' 'what I meant was . . .' 'what you don't understand . . .'

ACCEPTING PRAISE

To refuse praise reveals a desire to be praised twice over

Duc de la Rochefoucauld

People always remember criticism. They rarely remember praise or may reject it when it comes their way. Typically someone deflects praise with remarks such as 'it wasn't me, it was the team' or 'it wasn't difficult'.

You are being hostile, not modest, when you deflect praise. It's a way of rejecting the giver. When praise comes, listen to it. Simply say 'thank you'.

If you are trying to give praise and the receiver refuses to listen, stop the conversation. Say 'it's important you hear this'. Repeat the praise. Ask them if they have heard. Perhaps even ask them to repeat it to you.

Sam Goldwyn

When someone does something good applaud! You will make two people happy

GETTING DIVERTED

We often 'think' praise and criticisms about people, but seldom voice them, but we wonder why they haven't responded to our feedback. We need the courage to voice what we feel.

Equally useless is moaning, whinging and whispering behind people's backs. It might feel good at the time to share your criticisms with another person and get a resentment off your chest, but continued gossiping is a coward's way out. It doesn't allow others to grow from your comments.

It's the opposite of perfect feedback. In fact it's a perfect waste of time!

PART FOUR

Finally . . .

11

GETTING ON: PERFECT PRACTICE

You don't learn to ride a bike by reading about it. You have to go out there and do it. Knowledge isn't enough and it's the same with communication.

If a week after starting this book you are not practising, we suggest you're evading it. So start practising!

Apart from practice what mainly stops people improving their communication skills? Usually it's when they avoid building the relationships which eventually promote good communications.

So get involved. There are countless opportunities to test your skills. Earlier chapters provide exercises and information to help you. And you've already made the first step towards improving, by holding this book in your hand. The next step is . . .

. . . putting it down and practising

What are you doing right now? Are you at home, in a train, browsing in a shop, in a hotel, sitting in a car? Any moment now you'll be facing another live communication opportunity. It's another chance to practise – grab it!

So:

- Practise
- Assess your progress by staying aware of what happens while you practise
- Create opportunities to try out communication skills

- Welcome mistakes – even if occasionally they make you squirm – they're a chance to learn
- Keep digging into this book for ideas, exercises and encouragement

If you want to make a large shift you may like to seek extra help. It could be a workshop on negotiating, using your potential, self-expression, presentations and so on.

Sources for more help include:

Directory of Management Training
Your own professional body or association
The Good Counselling Guide
Association of Psychotherapists
Schools of Management
Local colleges
Institute of Directors
Institute of Personnel Management

One you may not have come across is 'The Mastery', a weekend workshop on self-expression and creativity, run by The Actors Institute in London. Our address is in this book too if you'd like a presentation or communication course.

Whatever you do . . .

. . . keep practising

And good luck.